Self-Driving Cars: "The Mother of All AI Projects"

Practical Advances in Artificial Intelligence (AI) and Machine Learning

Dr. Lance B. Eliot, MBA, PhD

Disclaimer: This book is presented solely for educational and entertainment purposes. The author and publisher are not offering it as legal, accounting, or other professional services advice. The author and publisher make no representations or warranties of any kind and assume no liabilities of any kind with respect to the accuracy or completeness of the contents and specifically disclaim any implied warranties of merchantability or fitness of use for a particular purpose. Neither the author nor the publisher shall be held liable or responsible to any person or entity with respect to any loss or incidental or consequential damages caused, or alleged to have been caused, directly or indirectly, by the information or programs contained herein. Every company is different and the advice and strategies contained herein may not be suitable for your situation.

DEDICATION

To my wonderful daughter, Lauren, and my wonderful son, Michael.

Forest fortuna adiuvat (from the Latin; good fortune favors the brave).

CONTENTS

Lance B. Eliot

ACKNOWLEDGMENTS

I have been the beneficiary of advice and counsel by many friends, colleagues, family, investors, and many others. I want to thank everyone that has aided me throughout my career. I write from the heart and the head, having experienced first-hand what it means to have others around you that support you during the good times and the tough times.

To Warren Bennis, one of my doctoral advisors and ultimately a colleague, I offer my deepest thanks and appreciation, especially for his calm and insightful wisdom and support.

To Mark Stevens and his generous efforts toward funding and supporting the USC Stevens Center for Innovation.

To Lloyd Greif and the USC Lloyd Greif Center for Entrepreneurial Studies for their ongoing encouragement of founders and entrepreneurs.

To Peter Drucker, William Wang, Aaron Levie, Peter Kim, Jon Kraft, Cindy Crawford, Jenny Ming, Steve Milligan, Chis Underwood, Frank Gehry, and Colonel Sanders, Buzz Aldrin, Steve Forbes, Bill Thompson, Dave Dillon, Alan Fuerstman, Larry Ellison, Jim Sinegal, John Sperling, Mark Stevenson, Anand Nallathambi, Thomas Barrack, Jr., and many other innovators and leaders that I have met and gained mightily from doing so.

Thanks to Ed Trainor, Kevin Anderson, James Hickey, Wendell Jones, Ken Harris, DuWayne Peterson, Mike Brown, Jim Thornton, Abhi Beniwal, Al Biland, John Nomura, Eliot Weinman, John Desmond, and many others for their unwavering support during my career.

And most of all thanks as always to Lauren and Michael, for their ongoing support and for having seen me writing and heard much of this material during the many months involved in writing it. To their patience and willingness to listen.

Lance B. Eliot

INTRODUCTION

This is a book about self-driving cars. Someday in the future, we'll all have self-driving cars and this book will perhaps seem antiquated, but right now, we are at the forefront of the self-driving car wave. Daily news bombards us with flashes of new announcements by one car maker or another and leaves the impression that within the next few weeks or maybe months that the self-driving car will be here. A casual non-technical reader would assume from these news flashes that in fact we must be on the cusp of a true self-driving car.

Here's a real news flash: We are still quite a distance from having a true self-driving car. It is years to go before we get there.

Why is that? Because a true self-driving car is akin to a moonshot. In the same manner that getting us to the moon was an incredible feat, likewise can it be said for achieving a true self-driving car. Anybody that suggests or even brashly states that the true self-driving car is nearly here should be viewed with great skepticism. Indeed, you'll see that I often tend to use the word "hogwash" or "crock" when I assess much of the decidedly *fake news* about self-driving cars. Those of us on the inside know that what is often reported to the outside is malarkey. Few of the insiders are willing to say so. I have no such hesitation.

Indeed, I've been writing a popular blog post about self-driving cars and hitting hard on those that try to wave their hands and pretend that we are on the imminent verge of true self-driving cars. For many years, I've been known as the AI Insider. Besides writing about AI, I also develop AI software. I do what I describe. It also gives me insights into what others that are doing AI are really doing versus what it is said they are doing.

Many faithful readers had asked me to pull together my insightful short essays and put them into a book, which you are now holding in your hands. I was trying to decide what title to give to the book, and fortunately something happened that prompted me to use the title you now see. Making a true self-driving car is "the mother of all AI projects" seems like an apt way

1

to describe this moonshot journey, and I explain in a moment what especially sparked me to use that title for this book.

For those of you that have been reading my essays over the years, this collection not only puts them together into one handy package, I also updated the essays and added new material. For those of you that are new to the topic of self-driving cars and AI, I hope you find these essays approachable and informative. I also tend to have a writing style with a bit of a voice, and so you'll see that I am times have a wry sense of humor and also like to poke at conformity.

As a former professor and founder of an AI research lab, I for many years wrote in the formal language of academic writing. I published in referred journals and served as an editor for several AI journals. This writing here is not of the nature, and I have adopted a different and more informal style for these essays. That being said, I also do mention from time-to-time more rigorous material on AI and encourage you all to dig into those deeper and more formal materials if so interested.

I am also an AI practitioner. This means that I write AI software for a living. Currently, I head-up the Cybernetics Self-Driving Car Institute, where we are developing AI software for self-driving cars. I am excited to also report that my son, also a software engineer, heads-up our Cybernetics Self-Driving Car Lab. What I have helped to start, and for which he is an integral part, ultimately he will carry long into the future after I have retired. My daughter, a marketing whiz, also is integral to our efforts as head of our Marketing group. She too will carry forward the legacy now being formulated.

For those of you that are reading this book and have a penchant for writing code, you might consider taking a look at the open source code available for self-driving cars. This is a handy place to start learning how to develop AI for self-driving cars. There are also many new educational courses spring forth.

There is a growing body of those wanting to learn about and develop self-driving cars, and a growing body of colleges, labs, and other avenues by which you can learn about self-driving cars.

This book will provide a foundation of aspects that I think will get you ready for those kinds of more advanced training opportunities. If you've already taken those classes, you'll likely find these essays especially interesting as they offer a perspective that I am betting few other instructors or faculty offered to you. These are challenging essays that ask you to think beyond the conventional about self-driving cars.

THE MOTHER OF ALL AI PROJECTS

In June 2017, Apple CEO Tim Cook came out and finally admitted that Apple has been working on a self-driving car. As you'll see in my essays, Apple was enmeshed in secrecy about their self-driving car efforts. We have only been able to read the tea leaves and guess at what Apple has been up to. The notion of an iCar has been floating for quite a while, and self-driving engineers and researchers have been signing tight-lipped Non-Disclosure Agreements (NDA's) to work on projects at Apple that were as shrouded in mystery as any military invasion plans might be.

Tim Cook said something that many others in the Artificial Intelligence (AI) field have been saying, namely, the creation of a self-driving car has got to be the mother of all AI projects. In other words, it is in fact a tremendous moonshot for AI. If a self-driving car can be crafted and the AI works as we hope, it means that we have made incredible strides with AI and that therefore it opens many other worlds of potential breakthrough accomplishments that AI can solve.

Is this hyperbole? Am I just trying to make AI seem like a miracle worker and so provide self-aggrandizing statements for those of us writing the AI software for self-driving cars? No, it is not hyperbole. Developing a true self-driving car is really, really, really hard to do. Let me take a moment to explain why. As a side note, I realize that the Apple CEO is known for at times uttering hyperbole, and he had previously said for example that the year 2012 was "the mother of all years," and he had said that the release of iOS 10 was "the mother of all releases" – all of which does suggest he likes to use the handy "mother of" expression. But, I assure you, in terms of true self-driving cars, he has hit the nail on the head. For sure.

When you think about a moonshot and how we got to the moon, there are some identifiable characteristics and those same aspects can be applied to creating a true self-driving car. You'll notice that I keep putting the word "true" in front of the self-driving car expression. I do so because as per my essay about the various levels of self-driving cars (see Chapter 3), there are some self-driving cars that are only somewhat of a self-driving car. The somewhat versions are ones that require a human driver to be ready to intervene. In my view, that's not a true self-driving car. A true self-driving car is one that requires no human driver intervention at all. It is a car that can entirely undertake via automation the driving task without any human driver needed. This is the essence of what is known as a Level 5 self-driving car. We are currently at the Level 2 and Level 3 mark, and not yet at Level 5.

3

Getting to the moon involved aspects such as having big stretch goals, incremental progress, experimentation, innovation, and so on. Let's review how this applied to the moonshot of the bygone era, and how it applies to the self-driving car moonshot of today.

Big Stretch Goal

Trying to take a human and deliver the human to the moon, and bring them back, safely, was an extremely large stretch goal at the time. No one knew whether it could be done. The technology wasn't available yet. The cost was huge. The determination would need to be fierce. Etc. To reach a Level 5 self-driving car is going to be the same. It is a big stretch goal. We can readily get to the Level 3, and we are able to see the Level 4 just up ahead, but a Level 5 is still an unknown as to if it is doable. It should eventually be doable and in the same way that we thought we'd eventually get to the moon, but when it will occur is a different story.

Incremental Progress

Getting to the moon did not happen overnight in one fell swoop. It took years and years of incremental progress to get there. Likewise for self-driving cars. Google has famously been striving to get to the Level 5, and pretty much been willing to forgo dealing with the intervening levels, but most of the other self-driving car makers are doing the incremental route. Let's get a good Level 2 and a somewhat Level 3 going. Then, let's improve the Level 3 and get a somewhat Level 4 going. Then, let's improve the Level 4 and finally arrive at a Level 5. This seems to be the prevalent way that we are going to achieve the true self-driving car.

Experimentation

You likely know that there were various experiments involved in perfecting the approach and technology to get to the moon. As per making incremental progress, we first tried to see if we could get a rocket to go into space and safety return, then put a monkey in there, then with a human, then we went all the way to the moon but didn't land, and finally we arrived at the mission that actually landed on the moon. Self-driving cars are the same way. We are doing simulations of self-driving cars. We do testing of self-driving cars on private land under controlled situations. We do testing of self-driving cars on public roadways, often having to meet regulatory requirements including for example having an engineer or equivalent in the car to take over the controls if needed. And so on. Experiments big and small are needed to figure out what works and what doesn't.

Innovation

There are already some advances in AI that are allowing us to progress toward self-driving cars (see Chapter 1). We are going to need even more advances. Innovation in all aspects of technology are going to be required to achieve a true self-driving car. By no means do we already have everything in-hand that we need to get there. Expect new inventions and new approaches, new algorithms, etc.

Setbacks

Most of the pundits are avoiding talking about potential setbacks in the progress toward self-driving cars. Getting to the moon involved many setbacks, some of which you never have heard of and were buried at the time so as to not dampen enthusiasm and funding for getting to the moon. A recurring theme in many of my included essays is that there are going to be setbacks as we try to arrive at a true self-driving car. Take a deep breath and be ready. I just hope the setbacks don't completely stop progress. I am sure that it will cause progress to alter in a manner that we've not yet seen in the self-driving car field. I liken the self-driving car of today to the excitement everyone had for Uber when it first got going. Today, we have a different view of Uber and with each passing day there are more regulations to the ride sharing business and more concerns raised. The darling child only stays a darling until finally that child acts up. It will happen the same with self-driving cars.

SELF-DRIVING CARS CHALLENGES

But what exactly makes things so hard to have a true self-driving car, you might be asking. You have seen cruise control for years and years. You've lately seen cars that can do parallel parking. You've seen YouTube videos of Tesla drivers that put their hands out the window as their car zooms along the highway, and seen to therefore be in a self-driving car. Aren't we just needing to put a few more sensors onto a car and then we'll have in-hand a true self-driving car? Nope.

Consider for a moment the nature of the driving task. We don't just let anyone at any age drive a car. Worldwide, most countries won't license a driver until the age of 18, though many do allow a learner's permit at the age of 15 or 16. Some suggest that a younger age would be physically too small to reach the controls of the car. Though this might be the case, we could easily adjust the controls to allow for younger aged and thus smaller stature. It's not their physical size that matters. It's their cognitive development that matters.

To drive a car, you need to be able to reason about the car, what the car can and cannot do. You need to know how to operate the car. You need to know about how other cars on the road drive. You need to know what is allowed in driving such as speed limits and driving within marked lanes. You need to be able to react to situations and be able to avoid getting into accidents. You need to ascertain when to hit your brakes, when to steer clear of a pedestrian, and how to keep from ramming that motorcyclist that just cut you off.

Many of us had taken courses on driving. We studied about driving and took driver training. We had to take a test and pass it to be able to drive. The point being that though most adults take the driving task for granted, and we often "mindlessly" drive our cars, there is a significant amount of cognitive effort that goes into driving a car. After a while, it becomes second nature. You don't especially think about how you drive, you just do it. But, if you watch a novice driver, say a teenager learning to drive, you suddenly realize that there is a lot more complexity to it than we seem to realize.

Furthermore, driving is a very serious task. I recall when my daughter and son first learned to drive. They are both very conscientious people. They wanted to make sure that whatever they did, they did well, and that they did not harm anyone. Every day, when you get into a car, it is probably around 4,000 pounds of hefty metal and plastics (about two tons), and it is a lethal weapon. Think about it. You drive down the street in an object that weighs two tons and with the engine it can accelerate and ram into anything you want to hit. The damage a car can inflict is very scary. Both my children were surprised that they were being given the right to maneuver this monster of a beast that could cause tremendous harm entirely by merely letting go of the steering wheel for a moment or taking your eyes off the road.

In fact, in the United States alone there are about 30,000 deaths per year by auto accidents, which is around 100 per day. Given that there are about 263 million cars in the United States, I am actually more amazed that the number of fatalities is not a lot higher. During my morning commute, I look at all the thousands of cars on the freeway around me, and I think that if all of them decided to go zombie and drive in a crazy maniac way, there would be many people dead. Somehow, incredibly, each day, most people drive relatively safely. To me, that's a miracle right there. Getting millions and millions of people to be safe and sane when behind the wheel of a two ton mobile object, it's a feat that we as a society should admire with pride.

So, hopefully you are in agreement that the driving task requires a great deal of cognition. You don't' need to be especially smart to drive a car, and we've done quite a bit to make car driving viable for even the average dolt. There isn't an IQ test that you need to take to drive a car. If you can read and write, and pass a test, you pretty much can legally drive a car. There are of course some that drive a car and are not legally permitted to do so, plus there are private areas such as farms where drivers are young, but for public roadways in the United States, you can be generally of average intelligence (or less) and be able to legally drive.

This though makes it seem like the cognitive effort must not be much. If the cognitive effort was truly hard, wouldn't we only have Einstein's that could drive a car? We have made sure to keep the driving task as simple as we can, by making the controls easy and relatively standardized, and by having roads that are relatively standardized, and so on. It is as though Disneyland has put their Autopia into the real-world, by us all as a society agreeing that roads will be a certain way, and we'll all abide by the various rules of driving.

A modest cognitive task by a human is still something that stymies AI. You certainly know that AI has been able to beat chess players and be good at other kinds of games. This type of narrow cognition is not what car driving is about. Car driving is much wider. It requires knowledge about the world, which a chess playing AI system does not need to know. The cognitive aspects of driving are on the one hand seemingly simple, but at the same time require layer upon layer of knowledge about cars, people, roads, rules, and a myriad of other "common sense" aspects. We don't have any AI systems today that have that same kind of breadth and depth of awareness and knowledge.

As revealed in my essays, the self-driving car of today is using trickery to do particular tasks. It is all very narrow in operation. Plus, it currently assumes that a human driver is ready to intervene. It is like a child that we have taught to stack blocks, but we are needed to be right there in case the child stacks them too high and they begin to fall over. AI of today is brittle, it is narrow, and it does not approach the cognitive abilities of humans. This is why the true self-driving car is somewhere out in the future.

Another aspect to the driving task is that it is not solely a mind exercise. You do need to use your senses to drive. You use your eyes a vision sensors to see the road ahead. You vision capability is like a streaming video, which your brain needs to continually analyze as you drive. Where is the road? Is there a pedestrian in the way? Is there another car ahead of you? Your senses are relying a flood of info to your brain. Self-driving cars are trying to do the same, by using cameras, radar, ultrasound, and lasers. This is an attempt at mimicking how humans have senses and sensory apparatus.

Thus, the driving task is mental and physical. You use your senses, you use your arms and legs to manipulate the controls of the car, and you use your brain to assess the sensory info and direct your limbs to act upon the controls of the car. This all happens instantly. If you've ever perhaps gotten something in your eye and only had one eye available to drive with, you suddenly realize how dependent upon vision you are. If you have a broken foot with a cast, you suddenly realize how hard it is to control the brake pedal and the accelerator. If you've taken medication and your brain is maybe sluggish, you suddenly realize how much mental strain is required to drive a car.

An AI system that plays chess only needs to be focused on playing chess. The physical aspects aren't important because usually a human moves the chess pieces or the chessboard is shown on an electronic display. Using AI for a more life-and-death task such as analyzing MRI images of patients, this again does not require physical capabilities and instead is done by examining images of bits.

Driving a car is a true life-and-death task. It is a use of AI that can easily and at any moment produce death. For those colleagues of mine that are developing this AI, as am I, we need to keep in mind the somber aspects of this. We are producing software that will have in its virtual hands the lives of the occupants of the car, and the lives of those in other nearby cars, and the lives of nearby pedestrians, etc. Chess is not usually a life-or-death matter.

Driving is all around us. Cars are everywhere. Most of today's AI applications involve only a small number of people. Or, they are behind the scenes and we as humans have other recourse if the AI messes up. AI that is driving a car at 80 miles per hour on a highway had better not mess up. The consequences are grave. Multiply this by the number of cars, if we could put magically self-driving into every car in the USA, we'd have AI running in the 263 million cars. That's a lot of AI spread around. This is AI on a massive scale that we are not doing today and that offers both promise and potential peril.

There are some that want AI for self-driving cars because they envision a world without any car accidents. They envision a world in which there is no car congestion and all cars cooperate with each other. These are wonderful utopian visions.

They are also very misleading. The adoption of self-driving cars is going to be incremental and not overnight. We cannot economically just junk all existing cars. Nor are we going to be able to affordably retrofit existing cars. It is more likely that self-driving cars will be built into new cars and that over many years of gradual replacement of existing cars that we'll see the mix of self-driving cars become substantial in the real-world.

In these essays, I have tried to offer technological insights without being overly technical in my description, and also blended the business, societal, and economic aspects too. Technologists need to consider the non-technological impacts of what they do. Non-technologists should be aware of what is being developed.

We all need to work together to collectively be prepared for the enormous disruption and transformative aspects of true self-driving cars. We all need to be involved in this mother of all AI projects.

WHAT THIS BOOK PROVIDES

What does this book provide to you? It introduces many of the key elements about self-driving cars and does so with an AI based perspective. I weave together technical and non-technical aspects, readily going from being concerned about the cognitive capabilities of the driving task and how the technology is embodying this into self-driving cars, and in the next breath I discuss the societal and economic aspects.

They are all intertwined because that's the way reality is. You cannot separate out the technology per se, and instead must consider it within the milieu of what is being invented and innovated, and do so with a mindset towards the contemporary mores and culture that shape what we are doing and what we hope to do.

Let's do a quick tour of the book.

In Chapter 1, I identify why self-driving cars are now becoming possible and popular. There is a grand convergence of technological, economic, societal, business, and other factors that have brought this to today's forefront.

In Chapter 2, though there are lots of ways that people refer to self-driving cars, such as by calling them automated vehicles, autonomous vehicles, driverless cars, and so on, I prefer to use the term self-driving cars. I explain my rationale for doing so.

In Chapter 3, I discuss one of the most important overall aspects about self-driving cars, namely the Society for Automotive Engineers (SAE) scale for measuring the capability of a self-driving car. I liken the scale to the famous Richter scale used for measuring earthquakes.

In Chapter 4, the advent of LIDAR is described, a key piece of the sensory puzzle for self-driving cars, though there are some that don't believe we really need LIDAR to succeed with self-driving cars. You decide.

In Chapter 5, my comments about how simplistic many of today's self-driving cars are has created some controversy and I address why I consider the current approach to be a pied piper method. It is something that won't stand-up to the rigors of real-world driving.

In Chapter 6, there is a discussion about how to watch out for videos that appear to show self-driving cars as miracles that can drive anywhere and in any manner that a human driver can. These sizzle reels are tricks. Watch out.

In Chapter 7, I tackle the ongoing series of public perception surveys about self-driving cars. Don't believe every poll that you see.

In Chapter 8, my concern about the rise of what seem to be self-driving shuttles is expressed and I debunk the idea that these self-driving shuttles are equivalent to self-driving cars. No, no, no.

In Chapter 9, I discuss the first of what I predict will be many class action lawsuits against the self-driving car makers. They are making bold claims and ultimately the lawyers will catch onto this.

In Chapter 10, the emergence of "fake news" about self-driving cars is addressed. Some of the fake news is by design and purposely meant to mislead, while other fake news is perhaps genuinely intended but written by those that don't really know what is going on. I try to set the record straight.

In Chapter 11, I tackle the rankings of self-driving car makers, which at times do not seem to take a fair and balanced approach to identifying what makes each self-driving car maker significant and how they will fare as we make further progress in this industry.

In Chapter 12, the aspects of product liability are laid out so that we can start to collectively have an open discussion about the safety of the self-driving car marketplace. I am betting that there will be some mighty product liability issues soon enough.

In Chapter 13, I discuss what happens when humans collide into a self-driving car. It's going to happen. Those that have their head in the sand and think that self-driving cars will avoid hitting people are blind to reality.

In Chapter 14, the elderly have been cited time and again as one of the biggest beneficiaries of the advent of self-driving cars. I agree that there are certain benefits, but I am not on the bandwagon in the same way that those with rosy glasses seem to be.

In Chapter 15, the role of simulations is described. Simulations are vital to making progress with self-driving cars. That being said, we also need to keep in mind the limitations of simulations and that ultimately actual road tests are crucial.

In Chapter 16, the seemingly crazy idea that self-driving cars could drive in a DUI drunken manner is presented. Some at first thought that I was kidding, but I am "dead" serious about this concern.

In Chapter 17, I bring up that there are human foibles when humans drive cars. Self-driving cars are going to be mixed with human driven cars for the foreseeable short-term, mid-term, and even long-term future. So, self-driving cars need to understand the crazy ways that humans drive, and then be ready to cope with the zaniness.

In Chapter 18, similar somewhat to Chapter 17, I dig more deeply into the defensive driving that any self-driving car worth its salt must be able to do. Most of today's self-driving cars don't do any significant defensive driving (that's a spoiler alert!).

In Chapter 19, I discuss an often heard debate at the self-driving car conferences about whether there is "one way" to do certain aspects of self-driving cars. Akin to the discussion about LIDAR, there are some that say the only viable sensor is the camera, and that somehow we can pretty much forget about dealing with radar, ultrasound, LIDAR, etc. I say hogwash.

In Chapter 20, the latest way that some self-driving car makers want to interact with a human driver is via the steering wheel. For levels of self-driving cars other than Level 5, the self-driving car will have to communicate with a ready-to-go human driver in the car. Augmenting the capabilities of the steering wheel is seen as one means to do so.

In Chapter 21, I bring up the interesting notion that maybe self-driving cars should be guided by a remote pilot, someone sitting in a remote location that can take over the controls of the car. This seems at first glance like it is sensible, namely, rather than having a human driver in a car to take over when the automation can't cope, why not have a seasoned driver sitting in a remote location that can do so. There are facets to this that aren't very attractive.

In Chapter 22, there is a frequently heard exhortation that with self-driving cars we'll be able to have "zero fatalities" and of which I say there is "zero chance" (kind of tongue in cheek, but nonetheless I mean sincerely).

In Chapter 23, similar to some of my other points about upcoming legal issues surrounding self-driving cars, I offer more such insights as a warning of what will occur as self-driving cars become pervasive in society.

In Chapter 24, I debunk some of the recent trickery of having self-driving trucks that appear to magically drive themselves across the country. This is mainly smoke and mirrors.

In Chapter 25, there is an important discussion about ethical aspects of self-driving cars. We are going to have self-driving cars that make decisions impacting the lives of those in the car and those outside of the car. We need to collectively be figuring out how we want self-driving cars to be making these decisions.

WHY THIS BOOK

I wrote this book to try and bring to the public view many aspects about self-driving cars that nobody seems to be discussing.

For business leaders that are either involved in making self-driving cars or that are going to leverage self-driving cars, I hope that this book will enlighten you as to the risks involved and ways in which you should be strategizing about how to deal with those risks.

For entrepreneurs, startups and other businesses that want to enter into the self-driving car market that is emerging, I hope this book sparks your interest in doing so, and provides some sense of what might be prudent to pursue.

For researchers that study self-driving cars, I hope this book spurs your interest in the risks and safety issues of self-driving cars, and also nudges you toward conducting research on those aspects.

For students in computer science or related disciplines, I hope this book will provide you with interesting and new ideas and material, for which you might conduct research or provide some career direction insights for you.

For AI companies and high-tech companies pursuing self-driving cars, this book will hopefully broaden your view beyond just the mere coding and development needed to make self-driving cars.

For all readers, I hope that you will find the material in this book to be stimulating. Some of it will be repetitive of things you already know. But I am pretty sure that you'll also find various eureka moments whereby you'll discover a new technique or approach that you had not earlier thought of. I am also betting that there will be material that forces you to rethink some of your current practices.

I am not saying you will suddenly have an epiphany and change what you are doing. I do think though that you will reconsider or perhaps revisit what you are doing.

For anyone choosing to use this book for teaching purposes, please take a look at my suggestions for doing so, as described in the Appendix. I have found the material handy in courses that I have taught, and likewise other faculty have told me that they have found the material handy, in some cases as extended readings and in other instances as a core part of their course (depending on the nature of the class).

In my writing for this book, I have tried carefully to blend both the practitioner and the academic styles of writing. It is not as dense as is typical academic journal writing, but at the same time offers depth by going into the nuances and trade-offs of various practices.

The word "deep" is in vogue today, meaning getting deeply into a subject or topic, and so is the word "unpack" which means to tease out the underlying aspects of a subject or topic. I have sought to offer material that addresses an issue or topic by going relatively deeply into it and make sure that it is well unpacked.

Finally, in any book about AI, it is difficult to use our everyday words without having some of them be misinterpreted. Specifically, it is easy to anthropomorphize AI. When I say that an AI system "knows" something, I do not want you to construe that the AI system has sentience and "knows" in the same way that humans do. They aren't that way, as yet. I have tried to use quotes around such words from time-to-time to emphasize that the words I am using should not be misinterpreted to ascribe true human intelligence to the AI systems that we know of today. If I used quotes around all such words, the book would be very difficult to read, and so I am doing so judiciously. Please keep that in mind as you read the material, thanks.

NEXT BOOK IS RELATED

If you find this material of interest, you might want to also see my next book, which also covers self-driving cars, but does so with a bit more technological flavor to it.

That book is entitled ***Advances in AI and Autonomous Vehicles for Self-Driving Cars*** and contains more of my at-times controversial and under-the-hood explorations about the nature of self-driving cars.

For readers wanting to go more deeply into AI, I have opted in that next book to examine aspects such as genetic algorithms, neural networks, machine learning, edge problems, cyber hacking of self-driving cars, and many other such topics. You don't especially need an advance understanding of AI to read and absorb the material. Those with an AI background will find it handy and interesting, I believe. Those without an AI background will grasp the essence and it might also put them on a path toward getting more immersed into the field of AI.

CHAPTER 1

GRAND CONVERGENCE EXPLAINS THE RISE OF SELF-DRIVING CARS

CHAPTER 1

GRAND CONVERGENCE EXPLAINS THE RISE OF SELF-DRIVING CARS

Why now?

As head of the Cybernetics Self-Driving Car Institute and a frequent speaker about self-driving cars and autonomous vehicles, I often get asked the question of why are we now seeing such a widespread interest and advancement in self-driving cars. Some inquirers feel that this is like suddenly discovering a new movie star and wonder what sparked that person to vault into stardom. Tagging onto that analogy, I explain that just like the proverbial small-time actor that starved and took on any off off-Broadway acting roles they could find, it has taken many years of toiling in research labs and universities that has preceded the now more visible appearance of self-driving cars.

Since the invention of the horseless carriage, there have been dreams of someday having a car that can drive itself. During the pre-computers era, attempts to develop a self-driving car were pretty much DOA (Dead on Arrival), since the kind of technological capability to achieve self-driving cars did not yet exist. During the early days of the introduction of computers, researchers realized that the potential for a self-driving car reasonably now existed, doing so by harnessing computers to act on behalf of a human driver. If you take a look at the body of literature on autonomous vehicles, you'll see that there have been hundreds of academic and research institutions and thousands of professors and researchers that have been pursuing the dream of a self-driving car for years and years. One of the most famous instigators towards self-driving cars has been the Department of Defense (DoD),

17

for obvious reasons of battlefield purposes, along with the DARPA sponsored competitions that have helped to push innovations in robotics forward immensely and that are directly pertinent to self-driving cars.

So, my first point is that it is not as though we all woke-up in the last year or two and suddenly decided to invent self-driving cars. The desire for a self-driving car has been around for a long time, and the advances toward it have been incrementally advancing. That being said, it has been a slow and snails paced progress toward a self-driving car. No overnight successes here. Inch by inch, we continue to make our way toward the self-driving car. I say this because some think that maybe there was a "silver bullet" that finally opened the door for a self-driving car to emerge. I know that some will claim that perhaps neural networks should be the winner for anointing self-driving cars as viable, while others would say that it is instead LIDAR (see Chapter 4 on LIDAR for self-driving cars), and some would offer other singular aspects of technology to assert that is the "it" that triggered the self-driving car craze.

Though it is often easiest to try and simplify the world and make the claim that one particular innovation led to a new world order, in this case I argue that anyone laying the credit at the feet of just one advancement is either ignorant about the field of self-driving cars, or miscomprehending things, or pushing a particular love-fest piece of high-tech, or has not taken a contemplative moment to reflect on what has taken place and continues to take place in the self-driving car arena. If you really step back and take a macroscopic look at the self-driving industry, you would come upon the notion that where we are today can be described in two words.

Grand convergence.

There, that says it all. It is a grand convergence. There have been a slew of key high-tech advances, combined with societal and business aspects, all of which have come together to create a circumstance and ecosystem that allows for the emergence of self-driving cars. Each of the members of this grand convergence have contributed mightily. No one in particular reins more supreme. At the same time, if some of the members were not present, it is questioned whether we would now be as far along as we are. Self-driving cars would still be toward infancy rather than maturing toward practical reality. Like links in a chain, each member of the grand convergence has made a contribution. Any contribution that had been missing would have left a missing link and we might not be at this pivotal juncture of nearing the realization of self-driving cars.

Allow me to also clarify that when I refer to self-driving cars, you need to know that there are an array of differences of meaning about what constitutes a self-driving car. As stated in Chapter 3 on the Richter scale of self-driving cars, we are only in the mid-way range of the levels of self-driving cars. Right now, self-driving cars are around levels 2 and just poking into level 3 (per the official SAE scale). We still have a fight on our hands to get to level 4. And, getting to level 5 is like a moonshot. Don't let anyone trick you into thinking otherwise. Even though each day there seems to be wild claims about a level 5 self-driving car coming upon us any day, it will be many more years before we see a true level 5 self-driving car. Mark my words!

What then are the members of the club of grand convergence? The membership includes various technologies. Technologies though must be understood within a context of existence. If I invent a better mousetrap, but the mousetrap is so expensive that no one can afford it, the technology will be waylaid until it somehow reaches a point of being more affordable. Thus, the technology must also be understood within a context of the social and business factors that allow for the technology to be deployed.

Here's my list of the members of the grand convergence that is leading us toward self-driving cars:

- Size of sensors

The sensors that go onto and into a self-driving car have been getting smaller and smaller. This is significant because they are easier to place onto and into a car, they add less weight, and they don't cause a car to become the size of a truck just to have the sensory capabilities needed to be a self-driving car. If you look at the self-driving cars of a few years ago, you can see how bulky those sensors once were. These sensors continue to be miniaturized and more readily used for self-driving cars.

- Price of sensors

The sensors for self-driving cars used to be immensely expensive, meaning that if you wanted to have a self-driving car that the cost of the sensors alone would make the price of the car be astronomical. In some cases, the sensors come to a million dollars in cost. Now that sensors are getting less expensive, it becomes more realistically viable to have an affordable self-driving car.

- Speed of sensors

The sensors for self-driving cars are getting faster and faster. The speed of capturing data is crucial since a car might be zooming along at 80 miles per hour and the self-driving car has to in real-time collect and process the data. We'll continue to see the sensors speed-up.

- Size of processors

If you wanted to put a vacuum tube based computer onto a car, you wouldn't even know there was a car underneath it. In that sense, the size of computers during the last 30-50 years has made a big difference in everything that is computer-based, including for example our cell phones. Likewise, the number of processors needed for a self-driving car is quite high, and so the miniaturization of processors is helping to make them available within self-driving cars.

- Price of processors

The cost of computer processing continues to drop dramatically. That's why we see them in the Internet of Things (IoT) too. Self-driving cars need gobs of processors, and so the decreasing price of processors is making this possible.

- Speed of processors

I feel the need, the need for speed. Processors inside a self-driving car are doing a lot. They need to analyze the sensory data. They need to run the AI software that allows the car to drive. All of this requires very fast processors if the self-driving car is going to contend with driving in real-world environments. Processors are getting faster and faster, fortunately.

- Internet connectivity

Some self-driving cars are independent of the Internet and don't need such interconnectivity to do what they do. On the other hand, it is more than likely that true self-driving cars will need to have some kind of interconnectivity, presumably via the Internet, but could be via some other means. Perhaps the most notable aspect of this would be the vast amount of data that a self-driving car is collecting and its ability to then share that with a centralized system, which can analyze it, and provide not only insights to the contributing self-driving car but also do likewise for a vast network of interconnected self-driving cars.

- Machine learning/AI

Within the field of AI, machine learning continues to provide capabilities to aid self-driving cars. The notion is that rather than trying to program explicitly whatever a self-driving car needs to know, we can have a self-driving car become "capable" by learning from data about driving. There are various techniques of machine learning which are now competing with each other to see which techniques provide the greatest benefit for advancing self-driving cars.

- Neural networks

Neural networks are one kind of machine learning type of technique and are perhaps the most known or discussed approach. This is an effort to try and mimic somewhat how the human brain works, by simulating neurons in a network like way. It used to be that simulating neural networks was hard to do in-the-large because of the computational processing needed, but with advances in processors we've been able to make this more possible. This is why for "deep learning" we can have much larger neural networks, of which the results are more impressive than were the earlier smaller or more shallow ones.

- Algorithms

You probably have heard that we are in the era of algorithms. Much of what runs our society on a computer based aspect is based on algorithms, ascertaining what actions should be taken by systems. Likewise, for self-driving cars, the advancement of algorithms and the ready availability has made them usable for self-driving cars.

- Big Data

To allow machine learning and also neural networks to do their thing you need data, lots of data. Advances in being able to collect, transform, process, and analyze Big Data has made self-driving cars "smarter" and more capable. A future key aspect involves data and machine learning for self-driving cars.

- Open Source

I know this member of the grand convergence, open source, might seem strange to those that are at the periphery of self-driving cars. What does open source have to do with self-driving cars, they ask. The open source world has brought into the fold many software developers that otherwise would never have known about or been able to contribute to the software of self-driving cars. To-date, much of the software was locked away in academic research libraries, or was held close to the vest by private self-driving car makers. This opening up of such software has led to more contributors and more advances in self-driving car than otherwise would have likely occurred. A burgeoning field is open source and self-driving cars.

- Automated Driver Assist Systems (ADAS)

We have grown-up with the ability to engage our cars into cruise control. Now, we have cars that can do parallel parking and other kinds of one-trick-pony car driving aspects. The advancement of ADAS is helping humans to get accustomed to having their car take-on self-driving car tasks. Those that develop ADAS see that they can get toward a self-driving car by expanding ADAS and making it more wholistic.

- Belief in Possibility

I would assert that a belief in being able to achieve self-driving cars is a crucial aspect underlying the advances in technology. If no researchers or developers thought it was a possibility, they would focus their energies elsewhere. By having a belief that it is possible, and that it is possible within a reasonable time frame, they are willing to devote their attention to this realm.

- Consumer Interest

Though you can invent technologies without caring whether consumers will have any interest in it, when you have a potential for widespread consumer interest, it helps to raise the stakes and get the attention of a myriad of inventors and developers. Consumers are primed to accept self-driving cars. They've seen the ADAS advances, and they want more.

- Investors

Money makes the world go around. Academic researchers that have toiled in self-driving cars have been scrapping together NSF grants and DoD grants for years have finally seen the spigot start to flow. Now, venture capitalists and other investors are agog about self-driving cars. The money is flowing. This drives the technologies and the technologists, since they can get the money needed to explore and experiment, plus they are certainly attracted to the potential for personal wealth.

- Herd Mentality

Self-driving cars cannot be invented by one person alone. The number of aspects of a self-driving car means that you need lots and lots of inventors and developers to each be contributing this or that piece of the larger puzzle. Fortunately, with a herd mentality that has taken place toward the advent of self-driving cars, you have enough of a widespread army of inventors and developers that each of the pieces is coming together.

- Applied Research

Foundational or basic research about self-driving cars has been augmented by applied research. Besides universities and colleges, we've seen a cottage industry of entrepreneurs that have now staked out space in the applied research toward self-driving cars.

- Google

You've got to give credit to Google for wanting to take-on the moonshot of self-driving cars, having been the first highly visible tech company to really take this seriously. That being said, they weren't being altruistic, since their efforts have obviously gotten them a tremendous amount of publicity over the years, and likely attracted other top high-tech talent to them, regardless whether that talent was immersed into any of the self-driving cars aspects. For Google, it was a good bet toward high-tech that might someday pay-off and that at the same time paid-off handsomely in publicity and attracting talent. They have now also spawned many former Googlers into helping to push along self-driving cars by having made the leap to other firms or going forth with their own new ventures.

- Tesla

Elon Musk is quite the character and his charm and publicity-getting attention has made the self-driving car craze what it is today. Tesla is a pioneer that has pushed forward on ADAS in a manner that we would likely not have had any of the conventional car makers try to do. Musk is a visionary that has taken a chance at spending on something earlier than most thought would make sense to do. The jury is still out whether Tesla will make the leap toward a true self-driving car, and some think maybe they'll get eclipsed. In any case, the Tesla remains a formidable challenger and something that has opened the eyes of the public, the investors, and the inventers about the strong possibilities of self-driving cars. Go, Elon, go.

- Media Frenzy

Self-driving car developers and inventors have pretty much been working in the shadows for many years. Not much interest by the media. A little bit of an advance here or there sometimes caught the attention of the media, for a moment. Without media coverage, it is hard to get a large preponderance of interest toward these advances and the technologies and technologies that make them happen. The media now seems to be in a frenzy to cover any and all advances of self-driving cars. I've though criticized some of that media coverage as being fake news, see Chapter 10 on that topic.

- Ride Sharing

What does ride sharing have to do with self-driving cars? You bet it has a lot do with self-driving cars. Ride sharing has brought to the forefront of our attention that we depend upon our cars and that there is a need for convenience of car access. With the billions of dollars that have flowed to ride sharing, it has coincided with the realization that if we had self-driving cars it would profoundly impact ride sharing. Ride sharing is helping to drive attention toward self-driving cars. See my article on the topic of blockchain and self-driving cars.

I have now laid out my list of the members of the grand convergence. Do you have other members you'd like to add to it? Be my guest. Do you believe that some of the member don't belong on the list? I think I've made a pretty strong case for each one, and keep in mind that I am not saying one is the most significant, I am saying they all had and have a contributory role toward the "sudden" appearance of self-driving cars.

Welcome to the bandwagon for self-driving cars. You can contribute too. No need to be a propeller head, since as you can see from my list, there are lots of ways in which the self-driving car realm is being formulated and grown. I hope that mainly I have dispelled the prevailing myth that there has been one factor alone that has led to the advent and now popularity of the self-driving car topic. There isn't a magic appearance of say penicillin or the breakthrough of the invention of fire that has been the silver bullet to make self-driving cars either possible or of interest. Furthermore, the grand convergence is so strong now that I doubt we'll see a fading of interest or advances. The appetite by everyone involved, inventors, investors, developers, media, consumers, regulators, and so on, has become so pronounced that we are now on our way to the moon, whether we want to get there or not, and we'll continue to see advances in self-driving cars, even if it takes longer than some of the pundits have been predicting. This train is underway and it isn't going to stop.

CHAPTER 2

HERE IS WHY WE NEED TO CALL THEM SELF-DRIVING CARS

CHAPTER 2

HERE IS WHY WE NEED TO CALL THEM SELF-DRIVING CARS

Stop for a moment and ponder this simple question. How do you refer to the newly emerging cars that are able to be driven by automation? Some call this automotive next-generation of cars by using the moniker of "self-driving cars" (it's what I prefer too, which I'll explain in a moment). Some refer to them as driverless cars. Others call them autonomous vehicles. A few people are calling them by the catchy acronym HAV's, which stands for Highly Automated Vehicles. I've also heard people utter exceedingly "science fiction" sounding phrases such as auto-piloted vehicles, and even the downright scary sounding robot-cars or the cooler version, robo-cars.

I realize that you might be thinking, does it really matter what we call them? Isn't a rose, a rose, by any other name? I emphatically argue that it does greatly matter what we call them. The names we use for things do matter. Many stakeholders are going to care about these mobile, AI-driven machines with wheels that cruise along our streets and highways. At first, it was mainly technologists that cared about them. Then, business persons cared about it, since the research labs where these futuristic cars were born have begun to see actual practical progress. Now, we've got politicians involved, regulators wanting to have a say, reporters weighing in about them, and the general public itself is queasy, excited, unsure and at times outright concerned about where these magical beasts are going to end-up being and doing on our roads.

Let's parse each one of these alternative ways to refer to self-driving cars. First, consider the phrase of "driverless cars" — I would assert that by using the word "driverless" you are making an important semantic mistake. You are suggesting that there is no one and even nothing that drives the car. Apparently, the car is just able to drive without any kind of intervention or control. Now, I know that those of you that are advocates for the phrase "driverless cars" will say, Lance, come on, the driverless part of things refers to the notion that there isn't a human driver involved. Further, those advocates would say it is "obvious" that a driverless car means that it is a car driven by a computer and it is implied that by saying driverless there is no human driver and thus who or what else could be driving the car other than a computer. To me, this is incredibly tortured logic. It requires us to make a mental leap that because it says "driverless" that it is really trying to say "human driverless car." I assure you that many people don't and aren't able to make that leap.

Furthermore, I think there is an even more sinister aspect to the driverless car naming. I believe it allows for a ready-made excuse for the automation that is driving the car. In other words, suppose a "driverless car" rams into a wall unexpectedly and not purposely. Well, some would say that's what you get if a car is driverless, i.e., there is nothing at all driving the car. It takes attention away from the real fact that there is something driving the car. There is automation driving the car. And it should be held responsible, which I mean to suggest that whomever wrote the system and put the system in place is responsible. By using the phrase "driverless cars" we are going along a slippery slope of forgetting and even hiding the fact that there is automation driving the car, and it, and those behind it, need to be accountable for what it does.

That's why I prefer to say self-driving cars. It immediately suggests that the car is able to drive itself. The car is doing the driving. There is a "self" driving the car, and it is generally obvious that it is not a human. Most instantly get the idea that self-driving means that the car has some kind of AI-based capability that allows it to do the driving of the car. This phrasing of self-driving car is a compact way to say it, using words that are easy to understand, and pretty much rolls off the tongue.

I promised that I would examine all the variants, and so now let's take a look at the other phrases. Calling these cars the phrase of "autonomous vehicles" has historically what they have been called in research labs. There is a tradition there. The reason why this isn't quite as useful as self-driving cars is that the word "autonomous" is one of those primped ten dollar words. I've seen non-technical people that have their eyes glaze over when they hear the word "autonomous" — it just sounds like a really big-time weighty word. I am not suggesting that the general public could not handle it, but just that it is the kind of word more naturally spoken by techies and less likely to catch-on in everyday use.

This brings up another facet, namely the aspect that the word "vehicle" is being used in the phase of autonomous vehicles. Again, this uses a rather formal word. Sure, people refer to their Department of Motor Vehicles (DMV), and so I realize that the word "vehicle" is accepted in general use, but I think that most people tend to say the word "car" rather than using the word "vehicle" when thinking about cars. Of course, autonomous vehicles is actually a broader terminology than saying self-driving cars, since the word "vehicle" could mean any kind of vehicle, whether a car, a motorcycle, and so on. I know that you might be worried that if we go with "self-driving car" as a phrase we will get stuck trying to come up with a name for motorcycles (self-driving motorcycle, autonomous motorcycles, headless motorcycles, or what?). We can cross that bridge when that day comes.

You can probably guess what I think of the Highly Automated Vehicles phrasing. Surprisingly, I do kind of like having a nifty acronym, in this case HAV, but I doubt it would catch-on. We already have HOV in common use, which refers to High-Occupancy Vehicle lanes, and I would wager a bet that if we also try to use HAV it will become confusing to everyone, i.e., did you mean to say HAV or HOV? I once again think the word "cars" is better for now, versus using the word "vehicles" and so I suppose we might aim for HAC (Highly Automated Cars). But, this is lacking too. By saying "highly automated" it is kind of a slippery way of being noncommittal about the automation. It is "highly" automated and so does that mean it can actually drive the car, or is it really just a cruise control kind of thing? Self-driving car beats out the HAV because you right away know what the automation can do, namely a self-driving car is able to self-drive that car!

The phrasing of robot-cars or robo-cars can be rejected outright. The use of the "robot" part of the phrasing makes us think of movies that have transformer-like robots, which we don't really have. If you were making a car that had a robot that actually walked and got into the car and drove it, then I suppose you might start saying robot-car or robo-car. Admittedly, there are robots that can indeed do that right now, in a limited way. Overall, though, that's not what we're going to see in self-driving cars. There will not be a robot in the front seat. All of the AI and computers will be hidden from view, stashed away in the engine compartment and other areas of the body of the car.

For the above reasons, I am an advocate of calling these new-fangled cars by the phrase of self-driving cars. It is the simplest, most elegant, catchy, and meaningful way to do so. The last phrase that I wanted to tackle is the "auto-pilot vehicle" phrase. What is wrong with saying auto-pilot? I think it perhaps overly anthropomorphizes the car. When you hear the word "pilot" you tend to think of an airplane pilot. Auto-pilot is already used widely for referring to airplanes. Most people don't really know what an auto-pilot system can and cannot do. Trying to reuse the word "auto-pilot" for cars is going to be confusing and also have people get muddled in what the vehicle automation is able to do.

The next time that you hear someone refer to self-driving cars, and if they use one of these other buzzwords, I hope you'll raise up your hand and offer to politely "correct" them about how they are referring to these new cars. At research labs, I realize many would not get caught dead using the phrase self-driving cars because it seems superficial and almost gutter-like. For them, I expect that the HAV or similar will continue to persist, which is fine. For most of the rest of the world, I anticipate that the self-driving car moniker will gain popularly and in a Darwinian fashion win out over other competing phrases. Either way, we should not call a rose by the name of sunflower, which would be confusing and I think that a rose should be called a rose. Just as a "self-driving car" should be referred to as a self-driving car.

CHAPTER 3

RICHTER SCALE FOR LEVELS

OF SELF-DRIVING CARS

CHAPTER 3

RICHTER SCALE FOR LEVELS OF SELF-DRIVING CARS

In the Los Angeles area, we get about 10,000 earthquakes each year. Ten thousand earthquakes! Yes, at first glance it seems like a tremendous number of earthquakes, and you would assume that we are continually having to grab hold of desks and chairs to be able to withstand the shaking. Not so. It turns out that very few of the earthquakes are of such a severity that we even are aware that an earthquake has occurred.

Charles Francis Richter provided in the 1930's a handy scale that assigns a magnitude number to quantify how much power an earthquake has. His now popular Richter-scale is logarithmic and starts essentially at zero (no earthquake), and then indicates that a 1.0 to 1.9 would be a micro-earthquake that is not felt or rarely felt, while a 2.0 to 2.9 measured quake would be one that is slightly felt by humans but that causes no damage to buildings and other structures, a 3.0 to 3.9 is often felt but rarely causes damage, a 4.0 to 4.9 is felt by most people via noticeable shaking and causes none to some minimal damage, a 5.0 to 5.9 is felt widely and has slight damage, etc. The Richter-scale has at the top of the magnitude scale a value of 9.0 or greater, and any such earthquake would tend to cause near total destruction in the area that it hits.

For Southern California, we get several hundred quakes that are around a 3.0 each year, and just a few larger ones annually such as about a dozen that are in the 4.0 range. When we get the "big" ones in a heavily populated area, perhaps in the high 4's, that's when you tend to hear about it on the news. The scale is not a linear scale and so keep in mind that a 4.0 is actually significantly higher in power than a 3.0. A linear scale is one that you could say that for each increase in the quake magnitude that the amount of impact would be relatively proportional for the increase. In contrast, the Richter-scale, since it is logarithmic, you should think of the increase as taking many jumps upward for each time that you boost the number, i.e., a 4.0 is many jumps upward from a 3.0, and a 5.0 is even more jumps upward from a 4.0. Another way to think of this is to imagine that say a 4.0 is to a 3.0 is like the number 40 is to the number 3 (more than ten times it), while a 5.0 to the number 3 would be like the number 500 to the number 3 (more than one hundred times it).

Why would you care about the Richter scale? I want to tell you about the ways in which we can measure the capabilities of a self-driving car, of which there is a popular scale used to do so, and in some ways it is analogous to the Richter scale. The self-driving car capabilities scale was developed by the Society for Automotive Engineers (SAE) and has been variously adopted by other entities and international and national governmental bodies including the U.S. Department of Transportation (DOT) and its National Highway Traffic Safety Administration (NHTSA). The latest SAE standard is known as the "J3016" which was originally released in October 2014 and then had an update in September 2016. The formal title for the standard is: "Taxonomy and Definitions for Terms Related to On-Road Motor Vehicle Automated Driving Systems."

Let's consider the nature of this SAE-provided self-driving car scale and its significance.

The scale ranges from 0 to 5, and is typically characterized as this:

Level 0: No automation

Level 1: Driver assistance

Level 2: Partial automation

Level 3: Conditional automation

Level 4: High automation

Level 5: Full automation

We don't assign intervening units within a level, and so it is always referred to as for example a Level 2 but not as a Level 2.1 or Level 2.6, instead it is just a level 2. This is therefore unlike how the Richter scale works.

With this SAE self-driving car scale, the levels are simple integers of 0, 1, 2, 3, 4, 5. The lowest value, the 0, means no automation, and the highest value, the 5, means the fullest automation. The values in-between, namely the 1, 2, 3, 4, are used to indicate increasingly added capabilities of automation. In that sense, the Richter scale is alike since as the numbers go up, the impact or significance goes up too. The SAE scale caps out at the value of 5, the topmost value.

The Richter scale is pretty much easily measured in that we can use seismographs to measure the ground shaking and then be able to state what the quake was in terms of magnitude. Unfortunately, similarly differentiating a self-driving car is not so readily determined. The criteria offered by the SAE allows us to somewhat decide whether a self-driving car is at a particular level, but there is not enough specificity and too much ambiguity that it is not as sure a thing that we can tag a particular self-driving car as absolutely being at a particular level. SAE emphasizes that their definitions are descriptive and not intended to be prescriptive. Also, they are aimed to be technical rather than legal (we will ultimately have lawsuits about whether a self-driving car is a particular level, mark my words!).

We cannot say for sure that a given self-driving car is exactly a specific level per se. Judgment comes to play. It depends upon what capabilities the self-driving car seems to have. We would need to closely inspect the self-driving car to ascertain whether it has the features needed to be classified as to a certain level. The features might be full-on and we could all generally agree that the self-driving car has the capability, or we might disagree about whether the features are entirely there or not, and if partially there then we might debate whether the self-driving car merits being classified as to the particular level.

Here's a bit more detail at each level:

Level 0: No automation, human driver required to operate at all times, human driver in full control.

Level 1: Driver assistance, automation adds layer of safety and comfort in very function-specific manner, human driver required for all critical functions, human driver in control.

Level 2: Partial automation, automation does some autonomous functions of two or more tasks, such as adaptive cruise control and automated lane changing, human driver in control.

Level 3: Conditional automation, automation undertakes various safety-critical driving functions in particular roadway conditions, human driver in partial control.

Level 4: High automation, automation performs all aspects of the dynamic driving task but only in defined use cases and under certain circumstances such as say snow or foul weather gives control back to human, human driver in partial control.

Level 5: Full automation, automation performs all aspects of the dynamic driving task in all roadway and environmental conditions, no human driver required or needed.

There is slipperiness in the levels 1, 2, 3, and 4, and so we will see self-driving car makers that will claim their self-driving car is at one of those levels and we'll need to collectively debate whether they are accurately depicting the capabilities of the self-driving car. A level 0 is relatively apparent and does not require much debate since it is a car that has no self-driving capabilities whatsoever. A level 5 is also relatively apparent (well, somewhat, as I discuss later on herein), since it is a self-driving car that can do anything a human driven car can do.

Whenever I hear anyone talking about self-driving cars, they often get muddled because they fail to differentiate what level of a self-driving car they are referring to. This is akin to referring to earthquakes but not also mentioning the magnitude. If I say to you that I endured an earthquake last week, what do you think that I mean? Did I experience a 9.0 that is utter destruction? Did I experience a 4.0 that is a somewhat hard shake with usually minimal damage? Or was it a 1.0 that I likely did not even feel and I am exaggerating about what happened? You don't know what I am referring to until I tell you the magnitude of the quake as per using the Richter scale. The same is the case about self-driving cars. If I tell you that I was taken around town by a self-driving car, you would be wise to ask me what level of self-driving car it was.

I was at an Autonomous Vehicle event, and there were some fellow speakers arguing vehemently about the present and future of self-driving cars. One was saying that we have self-driving cars today, while the other one was saying that we are years away from having self-driving cars. Who was right and who was wrong? Well, it depends upon what you mean by the phrase "self-driving cars." If you are allowing that a self-driving car is anything measured in the SAE levels of 0 to 5, then you could say that we do already have self-driving cars because we certainly have cars that are at the levels 0, 1, and 2. On the other hand, if you consider the only true self-driving car to be a level 5, then you would be correct in saying that we don't have any self-driving cars today since we don't yet have a level 5 self-driving car.

When talking with people that aren't involved in the self-driving car industry, I have found they are apt to refer to a self-driving car and be ambiguous about what they mean. Even most regulators and legislators are the same way. I usually try to make them aware that there is a scale, the SAE scale, and then inform them about it. Otherwise, without using some kind of scale like SAE's, you can have enormous confusion and nearly religious debates about belief in self-driving cars and doubt about self-driving cars, all because you aren't referring to the same things. A level 5 is completely different than a level 2, and so arguing blindly about "self-driving cars" is unproductive and exasperating until you state what level of self-driving car you mean.

One aspect that is sometimes used to make it easier to understand the levels of self-driving cars involves mentioning these three factors:

- **Eyes on the road**

- **Hands on the wheel**

- **Foot on the pedals**

At the higher levels of self-driving cars, you presumably can temporarily take your eyes off the road, you can temporarily take your hands off the wheel, and you can temporarily take your foot off the accelerator and brake pedals. Up until level 5, the human driver though is still considered the true driver of the car. Thus, even if you opt to temporarily take your eyes, hands, and feet off of the control of the car, in the end it is you the human that is still responsible for driving the car. I have exhorted in many venues that this is really a dangerous situation since the automation that suddenly hands control back to the human can catch the human unawares, and the ability for the human to react in time to save themselves from a deadly crash is measured often in split seconds and not sufficient for the human to properly take back control of the car. Also, humans get lazy and do not consider this temporary aspect of putting their eyes, hands, and feet afield of the controls as something that is "temporary" and will often start to read a book or otherwise become wholly disengaged from the driving of the car (leading to great danger).

A level 5 self-driving car is presumably one of the crispest of definitions since it indicates that a car must be able to be driven by the automation in all situations without the use of a human driver. Unlike level 4, which says that if the roadway or environmental conditions are especially harsh that the automation can give up and hand control over to the human, the level 5 requires that no human driver be needed at any time for any reason whatsoever. This is the ultimate in self-driving cars. We aren't there yet. We aren't even close, in my opinion. Achieving a level 5 self-driving car is the nirvana and something that is very, very, very, very hard to do.

This aspect of the level 5 being so hard to achieve is part of my basis for making a comparison to the Richter scale. Going from level 0 to level 1 is a significant jump, and so you might liken it to a logarithmic step up. Going from a 1 to 2, or a 2 to 3, or 3 to 4, those are sizable steps too, though it might be argued they are not logarithmic in scale. Going from a 4 to 5, it can be argued is logarithmic. This is due to the aspect that completely eliminating the need for any human driver is a really big step. A level 4 car might be pretty darned good, and you might say that well it just cannot do driving in snow or in a severe storm, but to me, until you have gotten a car to be driven fully by automation in all circumstances, it ain't a true self-driving car.

Google has been aiming at the level 5 and knows that it is one of those moonshot kind of initiatives. They eliminated any controls within the car, in order to make a bold statement that the human driver is not only not needed to drive the car, but that the human driver cannot drive the car even if they want to drive the car (since there aren't any controls to use). Many of the self-driving car makers are hopeful of eventually getting to a level 5 car, but for now, they are developing self-driving cars that are within the levels 2 to 4 range. Meanwhile, they have futuristic concept cars that show what the look-and-feel of a level 5 car might be in the future, but these concept cars are hollow and just something used to showcase design aspects.

Keep in mind that a self-driving car maker can skip levels if they want to do so. Some self-driving car makers are progressing from one level to the next, trying to achieve a level 2 before they get to a level 3, and achieve a level 3 before they get to a level 4, etc. There is no requirement they do it this way. You can skip a level if you like. Furthermore, your self-driving car might have some features of a lower level and other features of a higher level, and so it is a mixture and not readily categorized into just a particular level. As mentioned earlier, there is judgment involved in deciding whether a self-driving car has earned its claimed level. Ford has announced they are skipping level 3 and going straight to level 4, aiming to do so by the year 2021. Some self-driving car makers are predicting they will have a level 4/5 by the year 2019, but I am dubious whenever I see someone saying that they will be a dual level consisting of specifically levels 4 and 5, because as stated herein that a level 5 is a different beast and you either can do a level 5 or you cannot.

Indeed, we are likely to have "false" claims about a self-driving car in terms of the level it has achieved. I put the word false into quotes because a self-driving car maker might genuinely believe or want to believe that they have achieved a level, even though others might argue that the self-driving car has not achieved that level. The word false might suggest someone trying to be sneaky or nefarious, which could certainly happen, but it could also be done due to ambiguity of the definitions. Today, for example, most would agree that the Tesla self-driving cars are at a level 2. But, some claim that Tesla's self-driving cars are at 3. We can pretty much argue about this until the cows come home, and it is for me not much of an argument worth undertaking. We know and all agree that today's Tesla is not a 4 and not a 5, which therefore means it is quite a bit below what we envision a true self-driving car to be.

I don't want to seem like I am denigrating anything less than a 4. I do believe that we are pretty much going to be evolving self-driving cars from one level to the next. It makes sense to do things that way. If you are trying to bring self-driving cars to the market, you would typically bring any evolved features to the market as soon as you think you can. On the other hand, if you are doing as Google has been doing, which is more of a moonshot research project, you might not feel the need and nor the pressure to get the self-driving car into the market and thus will just keep pushing until you can get a level 5. We have though seen Google changing its posture on this, and perhaps realizing that getting into the market with their self-driving cars sooner rather than once they later on get to a level 5 might be a prudent thing to do.

For a level 5 self-driving car, some argue that the level 5 must not have any controls inside the car that would allow a human to drive a car. In other words, there isn't a steering wheel and there aren't pedals. There is no apparent physical means to allow a human to drive. The concept cars show that the humans are partying it up as passengers and there is no driver. The interior might have swiveling seats and the passengers can face each other, with no need to be looking forward and peering out the front windshield. The self-driving car is doing all the driving and so the interior compartment is just like a limo with no need for the passengers to care about the driving of the car.

This argument about the controls is open to ongoing debate. Suppose we did put controls inside the car, does it imply that the human driver is needed? Some say that no such implication is inferred. They say that humans might want to drive the car, and so they should be given the option to do so, if they wish to do so. By providing the normal steering wheel and pedals, it gives the human that option. The automation could still be one that is able to always drive the car, and there is never a need for a human to use those controls. Perhaps for nostalgia sake, a human might want to drive the car, or maybe they are a car buff and just enjoy driving.

The counter-argument is that if you put controls into a level 5 self-driving car then you are asking for trouble. The human driver might opt to take over the controls from the automation, but maybe the human is drunk, or maybe the human hasn't driven in years and is rusty in terms of driving, or maybe they take the controls over at the wrong moment just as the automation is doing a delicate maneuver. For those reasons, some say that a level 5 should never have any controls for a human driver.

There are also some that assert that maybe we go ahead and allow a human driver to drive if they choose to do so (not because they must), but they won't use conventional physical steering wheel and pedals to do so, and instead the human might use their voice to drive the car or use their smart phone or a touch screen to drive the car. Meanwhile, the self-driving car "utopia" people suggest that if you allow humans to drive in a level 5 car that you are going to mess-up the future when all cars are being self-driven by automation. Via automation, all cars will be able to communicate via automation and synchronize with each other in this utopian vision, while if you allow even one human to be a driver in a level 5 car then you will mess-up that utopia.

One of the current falsehoods, I assert, involves the claims that the self-driving cars are "safer" as you make your way up the levels. In other words, it is suggested that a level 4 self-driving car is safer than a level 3 self-driving car, and a level 3 is safer than a level 2. I think this is debatable. You need to keep in mind that all of the levels other than 5 will still have the human driver involved. Even if the automation is more sophisticated, you still have the human driver in the equation. Maybe you might claim that if the human driver is doing less as the levels get higher, the portion of the driving they aren't doing is getting safer, and so overall the stats will show that the safety has been increased. This is an argument that we'll need to see if it bears out. Also, even a level 5 cannot be seen has utterly safe per se, which I have covered in many of these essays the importance of self-driving cars and safety.

One technological aspect that is of fascination today is whether we know what kind of technology is needed to achieve a level 5 self-driving car. In Chapter 4, on LIDAR, I discussed that some believe you must have LIDAR to get to level 5, while others believe you won't need LIDAR to get there. Tesla claims that the hardware they have on their latest cars, consisting of 8 cameras and 12 ultrasonic sensors, and some other sensory devices and processors, will be sufficient for getting to a level 5. Don't know if this will be the case.

With the rapid advances in sensors and in processors, it could be that the hardware Tesla has today either will be insufficient to get to level 5, or might hold them back from getting to level 5. Given that they seem to be somewhat anchored to their hardware (entrenched due to investment), they might also see other more nimble self-driving car makers that adopt more modernized hardware as time evolves, and Tesla might be "stuck" with the older hardware that at one time seemed extremely state-of-the-art. We've seen companies do this many times in other industries, wherein they put a stake in the ground about the hardware, they get jammed up because of this, and others swoosh past them by adopting new hardware instead.

Another factor to consider about self-driving cars and their levels is whether you are referring to a pilot or prototype car, versus a self-driving car that actually is working on the public roadways. If I have a laboratory with an acre sized obstacle course and I have my self-driving car drive it, and I claim it is a level 5 self-driving car, does that really constitute a level 5? I would argue that it does not. To me, a level 5 is a self-driving car that can handle any situation that a human driver can drive, meaning driving in the suburbs, in the inner city, in the open road, and so on. A prototype that is able to make its way around an artificial driving course is not much proof in my book.

I would also suggest that we need the equivalent of a Turing test for self-driving cars at the level 5. Those of you into AI know that the Turing test consists of ascertaining whether you can differentiate the behavior of a system between what the AI does and what a human can do. In essence, if the system can do whatever a human can do, and if you can't ferret out that it is AI, you could then indicate that the AI is exhibiting artificial intelligence of the equivalence of human intelligence. This also means that you need to have a sophisticated human for comparison, because if you use a human that is not sophisticated you are then making a false comparison.

Likewise, for a self-driving car at the level 5, we are indicating that the automation must be able to drive in any situation that a human can. How far do we stretch this? A normal human driver is unlikely to be able to drive a car in extreme circumstances, such as on a race track at high speeds. Does the level 5 car need to be able to do that, or is it only required to do normal driving. There are human drivers that are inept at driving on ice. Does this exempt the level 5 car from being forced to show that it can drive on ice, since "humans" cannot do it either (or, at least some humans cannot). The nature and definition of human driver is itself ambiguous and so it leaves more room for interpretation about level 5 self-driving cars. I am prepared to propose a Turing test equivalent, and if anyone wants to then call it the Eliot test for self-driving cars, I'd be honored.

In any case, now you have an appreciation for what it means to be referring to a car as a self-driving car, and let's all be working toward the vaunted level 5.

CHAPTER 4

LIDAR AS SECRET SAUCE FOR SELF-DRIVING CARS

Lance B. Eliot

CHAPTER 4

LIDAR AS SECRET SAUCE
FOR SELF-DRIVING CARS

Is LIDAR the secret sauce for self-driving cars? I'll explain what LIDAR is, and also offer insights about the two different camps that fervently believe either that LIDAR is an absolute must for the advent of self-driving cars or believe that LIDAR is optional and likely overly expensive so as to not be needed for self-driving cars. Besides the technology underlying LIDAR and what it does, I'll also bring you into the world of mystery spying and intrigue that has recently been emerging around LIDAR as evidenced by the lawsuit between Google's Waymo and Uber, along with the recent ranking of self-driving car makers that put Tesla at 12th position, a much lower ranking than what most would assume and rated low due to Elon Musk's posturing that LIDAR is not needed. Get ready for a wild and engaging ride on the story of LIDAR.

Have you ever seen a picture of a Google self-driving car? If so, you'll notice that there is a kind of "hat" on the top of the car that looks like a flashing beacon or siren light, akin to what you might see on top of a fire truck or maybe an ambulance. Most people assume that this beacon or cylinder is there to warn other drivers that a self-driving car is in their midst. It seems almost like the kind of warning signs you see on a car being driven by a teenager that is learning to drive. Watch out, get out of the way, neophyte driver is here on the roads! Well, in the case of the Google self-driving car, you'd be wrong that the beacon is there for you. It is there to provide a crucial sensory capability to the self-driving AI, namely it is a device that emits a laser light beam and then receives a return that helps the system identify nearby objects that are out and around the car.

Called LIDAR, the beacon is an essential sensory device for most self-driving cars. It sits purposely on the top or roof of the car so as to have an unobstructed view. Originally called LIDAR as a mishmash of the words Light and Radar, it eventually became also known as Light Detection And Ranging, but some also refer to it as Light Imaging Detection And Ranging. You will also see it spelled in different ways, such as some people use LIDAR, while others use Lidar, LiDAR, LADAR, and other variations. Whatever way you want to spell it or say it, the end result is that it is a sensory device that emits a laser light beam which then gets back a reflection and can try to ascertain the distance between itself and whatever objects the light bounces off.

It is a range detector.

This range detector can be used to create a 3-dimensional mapping of what surrounds a self-driving car. The laser beam can be rotated in a circle, 360 degrees, and as it does so it is detecting the distances to nearby objects. The system then can reconstruct each of these range detections to try and create a kind of mental map of the surrounding area. There's a large standing object over to the right, and a squat object over to the left of the car. Piecing together a jigsaw of these puzzles pieces, the system figures out that the large standing object on the right is a telephone pole, and the squat object to the left is a fire hydrant. Once the system figures this out, it can then use higher-level logic to determine that it should avoid hitting the telephone pole and avoid hitting the fire hydrant, but it "knows" those objects are there and in case the self-driving car needs to take a sudden evasive maneuver and wants to go off-the-road to avoid a head-to-head car collision.

Rather than the laser beam rotating, modern versions use mirrors that rotate instead. This can speed-up the range detection and also allow for gathering more data at once. There are single-lens LIDAR and there are multi-lens LIDAR, of which the former is less expensive and easier to data process while the latter is more expensive and takes greater data processing to handle. The amount of algorithmic processing of the data being collected is tremendous. You need to get the data and reduce the noise and distortions, you need to do feature extraction to identify the skeletons of objects, you need to deal with the geometric facets and cope with the reflections from the objects, etc.

LIDAR has been around since the 1960s. This is a surprise to many in the self-driving car field since they seem to think that LIDAR was invented just for self-driving cars. Nope. It has been used for all kinds of purposes, and a great deal of the time was used in airborne applications. There are lots of terrestrial applications too, including for example in archaeology and for farming. This is pretty much tried and true technology. That being said, there are continual advances taking place. Let's discuss the impact of those advances.

One advancing aspect of LIDAR is that it is getting less expensive as a sensory device. The early versions on self-driving cars like Google's car were typically around $100K in cost (they were using a now older LIDAR model of Velodyne, a vendor that makes LIDAR's, and it was the HDL-64E LIDAR sensor at the time). As you can imagine, we are not going to have self-driving cars for the masses if the cost of one sensor alone on a self-driving car costs $100K. This would cause the cost of a self-driving car to go into the hundreds of thousands of dollars, after adding up all the other sensory devices and specialized software involved. Only the very wealthy could afford such a car. Furthermore, from the perspective of the car makers, they would only have a tiny market size to sell the self-driving car into. The Holy Grail of self-driving cars is to sell into the masses. There are currently around 250 million cars in the United States and about 1 billion cars worldwide. Car makers are eyeing that they could ultimately replace all those cars with self-driving cars and so that's a huge market. Game on!

Another advancing aspect of LIDAR is that it is getting better and faster. If you are dependent upon LIDAR as a means to guide a self-driving car, you need the LIDAR to work very quickly. Realizing that a car is moving along at say 80 mph, you need to have a sensory device that can grab the range detections in real-time, and accurately, so that the AI of the self-driving car can figure out what is going on. With each second that passes, your car has moved forward about 120 feet. Think about that for a moment. In one second, your car has moved forward over one hundred feet in distance. As your car moves along, it needs to rapidly ascertain what is ahead of it, what is the right, what is the left, and what is behind it.

Keep in mind too that the other objects around the self-driving car are not necessarily stationary, and thus you need to have the LIDAR detecting that another car is coming at you or veering toward you. The speed of the LIDAR detecting objects is crucial, since otherwise your self-driving car is "blind" as to what is happening. Suppose the LIDAR hiccups for even a brief second of time, it would be like you are driving your car and suddenly closing your eyes or look away from the road. This split-second diversion could cause a life-or-death aspect of your car hitting someone else or going into a ditch.

LIDAR is notorious for not being able to reliably detect close-in objects very well and so Google even mounted conventional radar black-boxes to the front and rear of their self-driving car. The LIDAR also can be obscured by other areas of the roof of the self-driving car, and so if you were to mount ski racks or something else on your self-driving car, you need to make sure that LIDAR still has an unobstructed view. Moisture in the air has often been troubling for LIDAR too. If there is rain, snow, or fog, it can cause the laser light to bounce oddly and so you won't get back clear and usable reflections from objects. This is gradually being dealt with in newer versions of LIDAR.

The speed of processing is also being enhanced. Some believe that conventional silicon-based chips can't handle in a speedy manner the huge volume of the range detections. Researchers and startup high-tech firms are exploring the use of Gallium nitride (GaN) transistors, which can potentially process at faster speeds than silicon. Price is a factor again, and so if you get faster in one tech but the cost goes up, you need to balance against slower tech that is less expensive. Indeed, there are LIDAR's that are down into the mere hundreds of dollars cost range, but those are slower and tend to be such low-resolution that few believe they are tenable for use in a true self-driving car scenario.

Now that I've covered the fundamentals about LIDAR and its use for self-driving cars, we can shift into the intrigue part of the story.

You might assume that everyone believes that LIDAR is necessary for self-driving cars. It is usually used in combination with cameras and other sensory devices such as conventional radar. You might think of this as a human that combines a multitude of their sensory capabilities for driving a car, such as your eyes, your ears, etc. The self-driving car fuses together the data from a multitude of sensors and then tries to map the world around the car and the AI then figures out what the car should be doing. Get ready to be shocked when I tell you who isn't using LIDAR.

Are you sitting down? Tesla is not using LIDAR. Furthermore, Tesla appears to have no interest in using LIDAR. According to Elon Musk, he doesn't believe that LIDAR is a capability needed for self-driving cars. His comments about LIDAR have drawn both criticism and praise. Those that praise his views believe that LIDAR is a misleading path and that we don't need it for self-driving cars. We can do what is needed with the other sensory devices, they say, and using LIDAR is unnecessary. Why bother with something that you don't need and will only increase the cost of the self-driving car? On the other hand, the camp that says LIDAR is essential is just about all the other self-driving car makers. Yes, Tesla is pretty much alone in their view that LIDAR is unnecessary.

Notice that Elon Musk has not said that LIDAR is bad or wrong. He believes that LIDAR is applicable for other kinds of applications, such as for his spaceships. He just doesn't think it is worthy for self-driving cars. Cynics say that he wants to avoid having to retrofit all of the existing Tesla's to have LIDAR, which would be quite costly. He will supposedly claim that LIDAR is not needed due to not having used it at the start, and now that he's far along on his self-driving cars that it would be costly and also look like he was "wrong" that he didn't earlier adopt LIDAR.

A recent ranking of self-driving car makers even put Tesla into the lowly position of 12th place, primarily because Tesla is not using LIDAR. The camp that believes in the importance of LIDAR has cheered this ranking and kind of thumbed their nose at Elon Musk. The camp that believes LIDAR is not needed has suggested that the ranking was biased by techies that favor LIDAR and so it is an unfair ranking. If you were ranking baseball batters and believed that the use of an aluminum bat was better than a wood bat, and your ranking was based on the type of bat used, you can imagine the rancor that would come out after the ranking was published. Does it really make a difference as to which bat you use? Shouldn't the batter be judged based on the outcome of their batting? Some believe that a ranking that assumes the use or non-use of LIDAR is a crucial factor ought to be tossed out, for the same logic as the use of the bat when ranking baseball batters seems questionable.

How important is LIDAR? You might have read in the mainstream media the lawsuit of Google's Waymo against Uber (it produced some headlines). In that lawsuit, a Google contends that self-driving car executive had left Google and founded a self-driving truck company, Otto, which was then bought up by Uber, and furthermore Google alleges that the former executive downloaded a bunch of documents before he left Google. Those documents were purportedly about LIDAR. Google is doing their own proprietary research into LIDAR and trying to advance LIDAR technology, which as I've mentioned here is an especially crucial element of the Google self-driving car strategy.

Recently, Uber went into court and denied that they have used anything that might have been taken from Google. Uber seems to be claiming that they could only find one document that might have been taken from Google, out of the alleged 14,000 that were supposedly taken. Uber also indicates that the Google research was about single-lens LIDAR, while Uber is forging ahead with multi-lens LIDAR, and so it is the case that Uber has not tried to leverage the Google propriety LIDAR, even if they had it, so Uber says. Uber has also tried the classic "their lawsuit is baseless" tactic by throwing other aspects into the mix. So far, the judge doesn't seem to be buying into Uber's positions and it appears that Uber is going to have a lot more explaining to do.

Beyond the intrigue, the point is that LIDAR is a secret sauce for some self-driving car makers. In fact, pretty much for nearly all of the self-driving car makers. The potential for LIDAR is gigantic in that if the preponderance of self-driving cars are built to require LIDAR, it will mean that you'll be needing LIDAR devices on ultimately say 250 million cars in the United States and maybe 1 billion cars worldwide. For those that see big dollars ahead, many are investing in LIDAR makers right now. This is a bit of a bet that you are taking, though, because if Tesla is right that we really don't need LIDAR for self-driving cars, ultimately the market will likely want to keep the cost of self-driving cars as low as possible, and so maybe chuck out the LIDAR due to its added cost. This is reminiscent of the 1980s when there was a war between Beta and VHS formats. For those that bet on VHS, they won, while those that betted on Beta took a hit. Should you load-up your stock portfolio with LIDAR makers? You decide, and about five to ten years from now, we'll know if you were right in your decision.

CHAPTER 5

PIED PIPER APPROACH
TO CAR FOLLOWING WITH
SELF-DRIVING CARS

Lance B. Eliot

CHAPTER 5
PIED PIPER APPROACH TO
CAR-FOLLOWING
WITH SELF-DRIVING CARS

Two major driving techniques are being used by today's self-driving cars; namely they look for lane markings to gauge where the road lane is, and they look at the car ahead to gauge appropriate forward motion. Let's consider these two techniques. Imagine that you are driving on the freeway and want to do the minimal effort needed to drive among the other cars that are the freeway with you. If you can identify the lane markings that are to the left and right of your car, and if you stay within those lane markings, you are able to proceed within a particular lane of the freeway. It is like being on a railroad track, except that you are merely using the lane boundaries as "virtual rails" to guide how you proceed. This provides you with a path. The other thing you need to know is how fast you can go. If you follow whatever car is ahead of you, and match their speed, you then have all that you need to get going. You have a path and you know how fast or slow you can go.

Suppose there isn't a car ahead of you? Well, you could proceed up to the maximum speed limit allowed. So, there you are, your car is on the freeway and you want to start on your journey. You look for and find the lane markings of your lane, and you stay within those, and then you accelerate until you reach the maximum allowed speed limit, but then go slower or faster depending upon the car ahead of you. As the car ahead of you slows down, you slow down. As the car ahead of you speeds up, you speed up. Often, a novice teenage driver that is learning to drive will use this same approach. It is a very simple way to drive. It works much of the time. You can strip away all the other cognitive capabilities of human driving and in many respects drive a car with just these two techniques of lane detection and car-following detection.

Does this always work? Absolutely not. There are limitations and dangers to both of these techniques. Furthermore, the combination of the two techniques is only a simplistic means of driving a car and can readily become fallible in everyday driving situations. The true Level-5 self-driving car could not be a self-driving car if it used only these two approaches. The lesser levels of Level 2 through 4 make use of these techniques and require that a human driver be ready to take over control of the car, precisely because these two techniques are insufficient to automatically have AI drive a car. The two techniques are deceptively convincing when you see today's self-driving car videos (see Chapter 6 about sizzle reels of self-driving cars). Do not be fooled. These monkey-see monkey-do kinds of AI driving techniques are extremely brittle, which means that they only function in narrow driving circumstances and once you change an aspect of the driving circumstance then these techniques fall apart for driving the car.

Let's see why these techniques are considered brittle. Suppose you are looking for lane markings and it turns out that the roadway is being repaired, thus, the lane markings are missing for stretch of the road. Human drivers usually are able to adjust to the situation and still pretty much make lanes, even if the pavement doesn't show it. For AI systems, this can be hard to do and they are apt to wander outside of the non-existent lanes that others are imagining are there. There are also cases of lane markings that have been placed incorrectly and so confuse the lane path. There are lane markings that are duplicative in that there might be old lane markings and new lane markings, so you have to decide which to follow. There are lane markings that are raised and readily apparent, but there are also lane markings that consist of flat painted indications that are faded and not so easy to see.

I'd like to though focus more so on the car-following technique and discuss how this kind of pied piper approach can be brittle too. With the car-following technique, you need to detect whether there is a car ahead of you. How far ahead of you is that car? What is its speed? You presumably want to keep a distance between you and the car ahead that is approximately at least the minimum stopping distance for the speed that you are going. If you are going along at 70 miles per hour, and if the car ahead is some X number of feet ahead of you, you can calculate how much distance you need to have in order to safely stop your car, if needed because the car ahead comes to a stop. This distance adjusts continually as you drive. You need to also include into your calculations the speed of the car ahead and how fast it can come to a stop.

We all do this kind of mental calculation every time we drive a car. A teenager that is learning to drive a car is warned to keep a certain number of car length distances away from the car ahead. You can see them driving on the freeway because they are the only car that has that open length ahead of them. Seasoned drivers tend to ignore the cautionary car-following distances and instead butt right up to other cars. This eliminates or certainly reduces available reaction time and more than likely means that if the car ahead slams on its brakes, the car-following is going to slam right into that car. We all routinely have that risk as we drive on the freeways today. Very few human drivers try to keep a proper distance from the car ahead. It is a game of chicken that we all play, each day. A novice driver discovers quickly that if they try to maintain the proper distance they will get honked at, and also other cars will jump into the open space and just keep cutting down the available stopping distance anyway.

For today's self-driving cars, they are programmed to be like that novice teenage driver. The AI is purposely attempting to maintain a proper distance for the stopping rules charts. This is impractical for driving among human drivers, since the human drivers are not going to usually abide by proper stopping distances. You can often spot a self-driving car by its distance following attempts, which can be just as obvious as when a teenage driver tries to do the same.

This raises an interesting and crucial question for self-driving car makers. Do you allow the AI to cut down on the proper amount of car-following distance, and thus violate the advised practices of safe driving? If so, and if that self-driving car gets into an accident because it lacked a properly designated safe distance, should the self-driving car maker be considered at fault? Lawyers are certainly going to make that argument and loudly proclaim that the self-driving car was driving in an unsafe manner. On the other hand, if the self-driving car is programmed to always and only drive with the safe distance approach, it can make it nearly impossible for the self-driving car because it is going to continually do a see-saw of trying to adjust to the car ahead and keep a driving distance that other nearby human drivers will continually violate.

This is why there are some purists of self-driving cars that bemoan the human driver being on the road. These purists point out that if we could make all cars become self-driving cars, the self-driving cars would all react to each other in the proper way, i.e., they would maintain proper driving distances. Indeed, one of the touted great advantages of self-driving cars is that they will be able to do a piped piper of long chains of car-following. Trucking companies are going to use car-following to guide many trucks on the same route, almost like putting train cars together in a long train. This also allows for greater fuel efficiency since the trucks can draft off each other. This all sounds good, but we are a long, long time away from having only and all self-driving cars and trucks on the roadways. The utopian world that these purists are dreaming about won't be here for decades.

Let's also consider some other drawbacks of the simplistic car-following technique. Have you ever driven on the autobahn in Germany and seen or heard about the massive car accidents? These are frequently caused by the aspect that cars are speeding along at very high speeds and one of the cars suddenly takes a dive. Maybe the car has a sudden flat tire. Maybe the car hits debris on the road. Maybe the driver just goes nuts and unexpectedly slams on the breaks. In any case, the leading car that suddenly comes to a halt catches the follower cars unawares. One by one, the follower cars ram into the car ahead of them. This continues sometimes with dozens of cars all piling up. In areas that have a lot of fog, you see the same thing happen. Cars ram into each other, not realizing that the car ahead has stopped or realizing it but not having time to react and avoid colliding with the car ahead.

The car-following technique has the potential for an adverse domino effect. Car after car can get wiped out, as they all ram into each other in a dominos-like way. In that sense, the car-following approach has both the positive of making it easy to drive and doing wind drafting off each other, but it also has the dangerous and severe consequences that you can have a lot of cars all become part of the same catastrophic accident. Some self-driving car makers point out that with the advent of V2V (Vehicle-to-Vehicle) communications, cars would be able to better protect against these domino effect accidents. Yes and no. Certainly having an ability for the cars to "talk" with each other is going to help reduce the risks, but it does not eliminate the risks. We still need to be aware of the dangers of the domino effect.

In terms of the leader role in the car-following scheme, let's consider some aspects of how this works:

1) Car leader maintaining speed.

If the car leader is maintaining its speed, this provides an easy effort for the car-follower since it can presumably aim to simply match the speed.

2) Car leader speeding up.

If the car leader is speeding up, the car follower presumably can and should do the same. The reason it should do the same is to maintain the distance between it and the car ahead. With human drivers, suppose the car leader is now going faster than the allowed speed limit. Should the self-driving car go as fast, but then be breaking the speed limit?

3) Car leader slowing down.

If the car leader is slowing down, the car follower would need to be slowing down, doing so at the same slowing down pace. This again is to maintain the distance between them. If this is a gradual slow down, then the car follower should also be doing the same gradual slow down. Suppose though that the car behind the car follower is not also slowing down? The car follower that is slowing due to the leader slowing can get hit from behind by a car that is not watching what is happening and runs right up upon the car follower. This can easily happen and a self-driving car needs to anticipate this (see Chapter 18 on the art of defensive driving for self-driving cars).

4) Car leader hits their brakes.

If the car leader suddenly hits their brakes, the car follower needs to do the same. That being the case, it is possible that the car follower might not come to a halt in time, and ram into the car leader. The car follower might need to take some other evasive action to avoid hitting the car leader, such as swerving around the car leader. Self-driving cars need to have this capability and not just blindly try to halt in the same lane as the car leader.

Consider that for each of the four above scenarios, we pretended that the car leader was a human driven car. These scenarios actually should be viewed as circumstances that could involve any variation of human driver cars and self-driving cars. In other words, we could have a car leader that is a human driven car, and be followed by a self-driving car. Or, we could have a leader that is a self-driving car that is being followed by a human driven car. The utopian world of all self-driving cars would be the scenario of the car leader being a self-driving car and the car follower a self-driving car. Today, we mainly have a car leader being driven by a human and the car follower being driven by a human.

In real-world circumstances, we are going to a combination of these scenarios as linked to each other. For example, we might designate that a human driver car is "HD" and a self-driving car is "SD" and thus have these configurations:

1. Car leader HD: Car follower SD
2. Car leader HD: Car follower HD
3. Car leader SD: Car follower HD
4. Car leader SD: Car follower SD

We can further extrapolate these to include more than just two cars. In a tighter notation, HD:SD would be a human driver car followed by a self-driving car, while HD:SD:HD would be a human driven car followed by a self-driving car followed by a human driven car. This notation allows us to then consider the variants of what each action might occur at the lead car and then what the follower cars might or might not do.

Some say that we should have a kind of master control of all cars on the road. If there was some all-controlling master system it would be able to orchestrate all cars and we'd never have accidents. I am not so sure that this is true, and even if it could be done we probably should question whether we want a master control to run our lives. The pied piper approach has some merits, but we need to be mindful of what it means for us all to be lemmings and whether that bodes well for us all.

CHAPTER 6

SIZZLE REEL TRICKERY
FOR
AI SELF-DRIVING CAR HYPE

CHAPTER 6
SIZZLE REEL TRICKERY FOR
AI SELF-DRIVING CAR HYPE

I've been speaking at several self-driving car conferences and noticed that the in-vogue thing to do is to show a video clip of a self-driving car in action. Various developers of self-driving cars are eager to showcase their self-driving car videos. Similar to something you might see at any car show, these videos depict a smooth ride and you watch in amazement that there isn't a human driver in the car. The video is usually shot from the backseat and so you have the perspective of looking out the windshield, and can see that there isn't a person seated behind the wheel. The steering wheel turns back and forth on its own, as though a ghost is sitting there. The movement and grace of the car appears to be akin to having famous race driver Mario Andretti behind the wheel, driving the car better than any average car jockey could drive it.

These are essentially sizzle reels. If you aren't familiar with the phrase "sizzle reel" it refers to a relatively short video, typically 3 to 5 minutes in length, and commonly is used for marketing purposes. Also known as a promotional video, pitch reel, montage video, or demo reel, these are usually produced with high-production values. In other words, the cost to make these short videos can be quite high, because the company using the reels considers it an essential form of marketing. If the short video doesn't get the viewer excited about the product or service, and if it doesn't look professionally made, it can lead to lost sales and buyers that won't buy.

Years ago, when I was an academic researcher in Autonomous Vehicles (AV), we'd make quite simple videos and show them among other fellow researchers. These had almost no production value and the camera work was shaky and often out-of-focus. Fellow researchers didn't care whether the video looked slick or not. Instead, we all were simply eager to see what the AV technology looked like and how it worked. Usually, the video would show not only what was working, but also show stuff that was being prototyped and so it might not be working or working incorrectly. We all knew that's the way that these kinds of advances occur. You try something, it flops, you fix it, you continue on.

Not anymore. Now, with everyone wanting to attract Venture Capital (VC) money to their self-driving car startup, the "research" video has morphed into a modern day ultra-slick sizzle reel. It pretty much makes sense because if you were to show a video to a VC and it showed your self-driving car driving down the road and, if all of a sudden it veers into a ditch, they'd be walking out of the room thinking you must have been crazy to waste their time on coming to see you.

I want to warn you about falling victim to these sizzle reels. It is easy to get sizzled, and believe that the video is showing you the real truth of what the self-driving car can do. I provide next some handy tips of how to be watchful of the trickery involved.

Misleading Editing. Most of these self-driving car sizzle reels do not show you the self-driving car over any lengthy period of time. This can be excused by the sizzle maker by pointing out that the video is only 3 to 5 minutes in length. This is true, but what it does is shows you only those clips that had the self-driving car working perfectly. If you saw a longer video, maybe one of a self-driving car on a several hours drive, I assure you that'd see imperfections as it violated some rule-of-the-road.

No Human Appears in the Car. These sizzle reels will usually omit things like the human test driver that is supposed to be in the car in case the AI fails in some fashion or cannot figure out what to do. For nearly all states in the USA, any self-driving car maker must get a permit to have the car go on the public roadways, and must agree to have a human driver in the car that can take over control of the car at a moment's notice. The human driver sometimes sits in the passenger seat next to the driver, but if you want to make a nifty video you instead have the human driver sit in the backseat, which then is not shown on camera because the camera is pointing forward from the backseat.

Crucial Omissions. The self-driving car will appear flawless in these videos. This is due to cutting out the video of the self-driving car when it inexplicably came to a sudden halt even though there wasn't any reason to do so. Or maybe the self-driving car ran a red light, but that was left on the cutting room floor. All of these imperfections are typically omitted.

Pristine Weather Conditions. Usually, the self-driving car will be driving during ideal weather conditions. It is a sunny day. There isn't any snow on the ground. You might not think about the weather conditions when you see the sizzle reel, and so you might mentally generalize that the self-driving car can work in any kind of weather condition. Don't bet on it. The worse the weather, the harder it is for a self-driving car. Most self-driving cars right now cannot handle adverse weather and expect the human driver to take over control.

Open Roadways Only. The self-driving car videos normally show the self-driving car as it is zooming along the highway. We are used to car commercials showing us the joys of escaping to the open roads. This same kind of imagery is handy for the self-driving car sizzle reels. What it is doing though is misleading you into thinking that the self-driving car can go anywhere. In fact, the toughest kind of driving is not the open roadway, which is exceedingly simple, but instead the inner city driving is the toughest. I think we all know instinctively that driving in an inner city with cars within inches of each other, pedestrians coming at you from all directions, bicycle riders, potholes, cars illegally parked, and so on has got to be the toughest driving situations. Sizzle reels usually don't show this.

No Nighttime Driving. Here's another harder kind of driving, namely driving at night. Think about how hard it can be to see the roadway ahead. Is that a pedestrian walking across the street or not? Where does the road curve? Most of the sizzle reels will only show the self-driving car at daylight. Don't be fooled into assuming it can equally drive at nighttime.

Purposeful Good-Driver Examples. This is the sneakiest of the sizzle reel elements. The video will show you a circumstance of a pedestrian that leaps from the sidewalk and the self-driving car magically comes to a halt. Proof that the self-driving car is not only good, but maybe even better than if a human driver was driving the car. This is usually sneaky because the self-driving car happened to encounter a circumstance that it was programmed to deal with. I am not suggesting that the makers hired a person to jump onto the roadway (which I suppose some might do), but I am saying that the self-driving car "knew" of that particular situation and so it dealt with it well. I would want to see other circumstances of when something happened that the AI did not anticipate, and see how it handled those situations.

Perfect Suburban Driving. Besides the open roadway, another handy aspect of these videos is they will show you a self-driving car driving in a suburban neighborhood. At first glance, it makes you believe that the self-driving car can handle inner city driving, since the suburb is seemingly similar. If you watch closely, you'll usually see very little traffic on the roadway and it is as though they picked a suburb from the old "Leave It To Beaver" television show. Try driving that self-driving car in a busy suburb first thing in the morning when every driver is striving to drop their kids at school and are driving in a panic to then get to work.

I want to emphasize that I appreciate seeing the sizzle reels and welcome that the self-driving car makers are trying to strut their stuff. A presentation that is only a PowerPoint with bullets, or just still images of a self-driving car, all of that is certainly much less interesting and informative in many ways in comparison to showing a video of the self-driving car in action.

What I am trying to point out is that we cannot allow ourselves to be misled by these sizzle reels and falsely believe that a self-driving car can do more than it realistically can do. Propaganda videos are good for getting people excited about self-driving cars, and can attract more talent and money to invest in self-driving cars. On the other hand, hyping what self-driving cars can do is going to have a boomerang impact. Ultimately, investors will get wise to these shenanigans. I am not advocating that we return to the old days of grainy videos that have cheap production values. Let's just try to restrain somewhat on the gee-golly wizardry of some of these sizzle reels. Keep the sizzle but add some reality.

CHAPTER 7

ROLLER COASTER PUBLIC PERCEPTION ABOUT AI SELF-DRIVING CARS

CHAPTER 7

ROLLER COASTER PUBLIC PERCEPTION ABOUT AI SELF-DRIVING CARS

Do you care about self-driving cars? If you are an AI specialist, the odds are that you care to some degree, since the hottest AI-action is right now taking place in the autonomous vehicles arena. Salaries and bonuses are humongous for those AI developers that are aiming at the self-driving vehicles market. Researchers that once were hidden in the basements of university labs and toiled away on driverless modes of transportation are now sought to create what some believe will be the most disruptive technological breakthrough in modern times. Auto makers are scrambling and rushing to get into this gold rush. All of the essays in this book have indicated a myriad of anticipated impacts on business, society, politics, and our way of living.

Does the general public care about self-driving cars? If so, what do they know about self-driving cars, or, rather what do they think that they know? Much of the public perception about self-driving cars is based on a combination of real news and fake news (see Chapter 10 covering the fake news and its impacts). The public gets glimpses of what is happening with self-driving cars as fed to them by occasional coverage in the major media outlets. Remember the pretend game you did as a child involving closing your eyes and then randomly opening to see what is going on, and then trying to piece together the reality by those short snippets? That's what the public is doing today.

Recent polls are trying figure out the nature of public opinion regarding self-driving cars. Seems like we see a new poll every week. In some cases, the poll sways the voting by portraying self-driving cars as either savior of goodness or as evil doomsayers. You can get the public to pretty much go in a particular direction by how you phrase the questions. It's similar to polls done for political races. If I ask you whether you support James Smith for president, I've worded the question in a relatively neutral fashion. If I instead ask you whether you support a lying, cheating, horse stealing James Smith for president, I have loaded the question in a direction that is likely to get you to say no. I might instead ask whether you want the gallant, honorable, hero James Smith to be president, and you'll shift toward saying yes. Of course, some people will already have a predetermined opinion regardless of how the question is worded, but those that are on-the-fence or not in the know can be maneuvered by how the question is phrased.

I tell you this aspect because I'd ask that you gauge the results of public surveys about self-driving cars with a grain of salt. A headline that announces the public is eager to have self-driving cars can be inherently biased by perhaps asking whether someone wants a self-driving car that will save lives and reduce pollutants. Who can disagree with that kind of question? Not many. On the other hand, if the survey asked whether you want self-driving cars that will endanger lives, drive recklessly, and start us toward a future of AI taking over the world, I am betting that most would insist they don't want self-driving cars. Trickery by the designer of the survey is just as much a part of the survey as anything else that the survey purports to do or say.

Not only is the survey design crucial, it is also important to consider to whom the survey is administered. If I give a survey about self-driving cars to researchers and AI specialists, I'll likely get a result that would differ from giving the same survey to teenagers in high school. There's a famous case about survey selection problems that took place during the presidential election in 1936. A popular magazine called The Literary Digest sampled 2.4 million Americans to then predict which candidate would win the presidential vote. Turns out The Literary Digest prediction was wrong, and led to a shocking surprise since it was one of the largest sized samples ever done for a national poll. How did they get it wrong? They selected names by looking at their subscribers and telephone directories, primarily of which were higher income and white. This is known as selection bias. They also originally put together a list of 10 million names, but only those that actually responded to the survey were the 2.4 million people. This is a nonresponse bias that meant only those that did respond cast an opinion, while the millions of others that did not respond we have no idea what their opinion might be.

Be careful therefore in believing any self-driving car poll that you see. Some of the polls are done by professional survey experts that know how to properly design and conduct a survey, and for those polls I would gauge that we can generally accept their results. Other polls that are done ad hoc by someone that knows nothing about properly doing polls should be considered highly suspect. There are also some polls that want to get a particular answer, and so those pollsters will then purposely shape the questions and the selection of respondents to get the outcome they want. If you are an organization that wants to bash self-driving cars, you can easily create a poll that gets that kind of public perception results. If you are an organization that wants the public perception to seemingly be that self-driving cars are essential, you can get that response by how you develop the survey.

Let's take a look at a specific poll that was recently undertaken and gained national and international attention and was undertaken by the American Automobile Association (AAA). The American Automobile Association is a well-known entity that provides various auto related services to consumers. The Triple-A, as it is informally called, consists of a federation of automobile clubs throughout North America and has a membership of around 50-60 million consumers, which is a hefty and very impressive number (the AAA has a lot of clout due to this count). Besides providing roadside assistance, the AAA also provides help in all forms of travel, car insurance, tourism info for places you might go visit, and the like. As you might guess, they have a big stake too in the advent of self-driving cars. Right now, most of their membership consists of drivers. This is a significant in that their bread and butter is due to drivers — keep in mind that if there are less people driving due to the arrival of self-driving cars, it could dramatically impact the AAA as an entity and its survival. Some believe that the AAA will have to radically transform itself to adjust to a predominantly passengers-only world of self-driving cars.

The AAA did a survey in January 2017 about self-driving cars and released Phase 2 of the results in March 2017. I am hoping you already are wondering how the questions were worded, and also wondering whom they opted to survey (if you've been paying attention to my raving and ranting in this piece). As forewarned, knowing those aspects is crucial to being able to interpret the results of a survey and also what kind of biases might have been purposely or accidentally embedded in the polling. In this case, they randomly selected landline phone numbers and also mobile cell phone numbers of 1,012 adults (ages 18 and over) that were living in the continental United States at the time of the polling. I won't get into further details about their methodology here and urge you to take a look at the AAA published poll to see the other various assumptions and limitations.

The result that got the most headlines by the AAA consisted of the "finding" that 75% or three-quarters of United States drivers said they were afraid to ride in a self-driving car. We can readily quibble with this finding due to how they asked the question and also the sampling choices used. I am not going to fight that battle here, and instead pretend that the result is bona fide. As such, what does it mean?

Suppose you believe that self-driving cars are safe. Your interpretation of the aspect that 75% of drivers are fearful shows that the public is quite confused and they plainly don't know what they are talking about. Perhaps they are naïve. Perhaps they think of self-driving cars like Frankenstein and so have a mistaken view of what self-driving cars are. Scientists often find that the public lags awareness of scientific breakthroughs and can be hesitant to embrace new innovations.

Suppose you believe that self-driving cars are not safe. Your interpretation of the 75% result is that thankfully American drivers are astute enough to know that they should be wary of self-driving cars. Whether these people knew what they were saying, or were just basing their opinion on a hunch, they got it right. This can be used to prod the self-driving car makers into being more focused on the safety aspects of self-driving cars. It also enables politicians to put in place regulations about self-driving cars, which they can say is being done due to overwhelming public opinion that self-driving cars are perceived not to be safe.

There are some additional results that you might find of interest, and that might also make your blood boil, depending upon your stance about self-driving cars. The poll indicated that women tended to be more afraid than men about riding in self-driving cars (85% of women versus 69% of men). Some might say that this is because women are likely to be more fearful of mechanical things (there's a misogynist view for you!), while others might say that women are more enlightened and less willing to blindly believe that these self-driving cars are safe (men let their bravado do their thinking for them).

The survey also reported that if you divide the respondents into Millennials (ages 18-36), Generation X (ages 37-52), and Baby Boomers (ages 53-71), the group that was more fearful was Baby Boomers (85%), then Generation X (75%), and then Millennials (73%). We might use the politically Impolite aspects of ageism and declare that the oldies "don't get" new technology, while the youngsters do. On the other hand, some might say that the elders have wisdom that they've seen many a technology that was over-hyped and turned out to be worse than we were being told.

If you are a self-driving car maker, and if you believe this poll, the point for you is that you need to do something to get the public to believe in self-driving cars. I suppose you could jack-up the belief in self-driving cars by getting some hot celebrity to go around in a self-driving car. You could do a marketing campaign about how unsafe human drivers are, and thus get the public to de facto assume that self-driving cars must be safer. And so on.

Another question asked by the poll involved whether human drivers feel safe around self-driving cars, when both are on the road together. Now, you would almost assume that if 75% don't feel safe being in a self-driving car, they certainly would also not feel safe being near one on the road. In fact, you would probably assume that an even higher percentage would say that they don't trust the self-driving cars to be mixed with the human drivers. Well, you'd be wrong. Turns out that only about half or 54% said they would feel less safe sharing the road with self-driving cars. I guess the logic must be that as a human driver in your own car that you can avoid the unsafe nature of the self-driving car nearby, but if you are actually in a self-driving car then you are stuck at the whim of the unsafe self-driving car. Or something like that.

The last item that I'll cover about this poll consists of a question asked about how the public perceives the nature of the autonomous systems that would be on these self-driving cars. According to the poll, approximately 8 of 10 said that they want the autonomous systems to work in the same way (81% said so), irrespective of which car maker provides the features. This is not exclusively about self-driving cars per se, since the question defined the autonomous systems to include lane keeping, adaptive cruise control, self-parking, automatic emergency braking, and so on. It certainly makes sense that people would want these features to be consistent across car makers and models.

I've already written about the aspect that at first we're going to see the car makers using their self-driving car capabilities as a means to differentiate themselves in the marketplace. No auto maker that has spent billions of dollars is going to like the idea that all self-driving cars do the same thing. Instead, they each want to have their own competitive advantage. For consumers, it will be the wild west of trying to figure out what one auto maker has versus another. Is the self-driving capabilities of a Ford any better or worse than those of a Toyota? And, how can the consumer know for sure, other than the massive advertising that will be done by the auto makers. Entities like the AAA will be looked upon by consumers to help them figure out what is the truth about the auto makers claims.

Overall, these polls are handy to try and ascertain what the public thinks about self-driving cars. Please don't believe a poll simply because it seems to agree with your own opinion. Look under the hood, so to speak, and see what the survey design consisted of and how they respondents were selected and contacted. If the survey results disagree with your opinion, don't immediately reject the survey, and instead take a closer look at how it was undertaken. You might know that there's a famous line about statistics, which was uttered by British Prime Minister Benjamin Disraeli: "There are three kinds of lies: lies, damned lies, and statistics." For those that believe in the future of self-driving cars, if we see polls that seem overly distorted and misrepresent self-driving cars, we'll need to speak out. At the same time, we cannot discount public perceptions, even if it is poorly informed, as we presumably should help shoulder the responsibility to properly inform the public about the present and future of AI and self-driving cars. One thing for sure, we're likely to see public perception rise and fall, one moment loving AI self-driving cars and the next trouncing them. It will be a roller coaster ride of public perception. Keep your eyes wide open, and make sure to buckle up!

CHAPTER 8

BRAINLESS SELF-DRIVING SHUTTLES ARE NOT THE SAME AS AI SELF-DRIVING CARS

CHAPTER 8

BRAINLESS SELF-DRIVING SHUTTLES ARE NOT THE SAME AS AI SELF-DRIVING CARS

Senator, you're no Jack Kennedy.

That's a famous line that was uttered by Senator Lloyd Bentsen during the Vice-Presidential candidate debate against Senator Dan Quayle in 1988. During the debate, Dan Quayle had somewhat equated himself to the heroics and stature of former President Jack Kennedy. Lloyd Bentsen struck back with the biting words that as someone that knew Jack Kennedy, and given the achievements of Jack Kennedy, in no manner whatsoever could Dan Quayle be considered the equivalent. It was a remark that served to cut down Dan Quayle and vaulted Lloyd Bentsen into the famous quotes stratosphere. The same kind of line is used today in both everyday conversation and in political stump speeches, and used to cut down an opponent during a discussion or outright debate. Having incredible stickiness and memorable as a slur, anyone today needs to be cautious in trying to compare themselves to something or someone else that is great, because your opponent can trot out a variation of the "you're no" and do the contemporary drop-the-microphone to win the debate.

Why do I dredge up this notable line? Because there are some that want to equate the recent emergence of self-driving shuttle vans to the emergence of AI self-driving cars. By-and-large, this is a misleading comparison. These self-driving shuttle vans are usually a shallow version of what a true self-driving car is supposed to be and do. I'll explain why the comparison is so misleading. Worse too, it has the

79

danger of confusing the public about the nature of self-driving cars. In the same breath, it will actually have some positive impacts on self-driving cars and so I'll cover that too. Overall, though, I'd like to clearly state this: I know all about AI self-driving cars, I have been writing all about AI self-driving cars, and I can say that the emerging self-driving shuttles are "not Jack Kennedy" as in they are not AI self-driving cars.

A recent rumor is that Walt Disney World is going to deploy self-driving shuttle vans at their resort properties in Florida. It is said that either or both of Local Motors (Phoenix) and Navya (Paris) might supply the shuttles. Disney will presumably do an initial series of tests, likely using "cast members" (Disney employees) as the initial passengers in the vehicles. If you've ever been to the massive properties that Disney has in Florida, you well know the need to have shuttles that take you throughout their resort locations. Distances between their theme parks, restaurants, hotels, and other venues can be in the dozens of miles. Already there is a small army of shuttles, buses, boats, and all manner of transport provided. There several monorails too, along with bike rentals and rickshaw modes of transportation. Thousands upon thousands of guests and employees are in constant motion inside and throughout the properties. It is like a massive ant farm.

Currently, the manpower needed to undertake all this transportation is enormous. Zillions of human drivers are needed. They need to be trained in how to drive the vehicles. They need to be available and be at their assigned vehicles when needed. They need to be in their right-mind and not distracted or somehow say drunk or otherwise unable to properly drive. Some will be sick on given day or shift, or play hooky and not show-up for work. Substitutes need to be ready to step-in. All those drivers need to be supervised and monitored. They need to be responsive to changes in schedules and changes in routes. At times, they interact with guests and so need to showcase themselves in a Disneyesque way of being pleasant and friendly.

In short, from a management perspective, it's a nightmare. The logistics is sizable and it is a daily chore of ensuring that things go right. If transportation goes sour, the guests go sour. If the guests go sour, the resort loses the guests. If the resort loses the guests, the revenue drops. The transportation is not something that you might at first think is crucial to the success of the Disney parks there, but it is. Transporting people is one of those seemingly hidden aspects that until you have a transportation glitch or stoppage you just take it for granted. The Disney locations in Orlando are especially vulnerable since they are so spread out. In contrast, the Disneyland resort in Anaheim, California is much more compact and the transportation aspects are not nearly as vital to the ongoing operations there.

Without a doubt, it makes a lot of sense for Disney to want to use self-driving shuttles at their Florida parks. No human drivers means that you can wipe out all the troubles and costs of having those human drivers. No need to worry whether the driver will show-up for their shift. No need to worry whether the driver is alert and aware while driving the guests. Consider all the labor costs of regular time and overtime that is needed to keep the transportation going. Knock down that cost and the savings are impressive. It is pretty much a no-brainer that if you could get rid of the drivers you would be better off in nearly all respects.

I know you might say that the drivers are human ambassadors and that guests are enchanted by their smiles and pleasantries. Yes and no. Getting a human driver to be smiling and pleasant is a hard thing to do. They might hate their job and take it out on the guests. They might have had a bad day and are taking it out on the guests. They might get verbally abused by a guest and then take it out on other guests. There is no guarantee that the drivers are going to be good human ambassadors. Meanwhile, if the robotic shuttle has some kind of pre-recorded super-friendly voices that emit messages and funny anecdotes, the odds are that guests will as enchanted as they would be a human driver, and also that Disney will avoid the dangers of those human drivers that treat the guests poorly.

Think about this aspect of using self-driving shuttles and you realize that Disney can also capitalize on their Tomorrowland type atmosphere. People love to ride on the monorails because it gives them a sense of what the future is supposed to be. Remember when you were a child and the entire world was supposed to eventually have those slick, safe, and clean monorails? Sorry, we are still not there. But, anyway, guests going to the parks will likely love to ride on the self-driving shuttles. It is another added "magical ride" at the resorts and will portray Disney as once again an innovator that is trying to paint a bright and better future. I am betting that acceptance by guests will be high, the costs for providing the transportation will drop, and even likely the transportation will run more smoothly overall. The loss of jobs for the human drivers will hurt, and there will likely be attempts by labor to curtail or stop the onslaught of the self-driving shuttles, yet it is unlikely that the affected labor can muster enough of a protest to prevent the conversion.

Let's get back to my original premise about the nature of these self-driving shuttles. I wanted to emphasize that they are not the same as AI self-driving cars. Someday in the future they might be, but the ones that are rolling out in the foreseeable future are pretty much brainless. First, we'll consider the simple physical aspects of the shuttles. A typical self-driving shuttle holds about a dozen or so passengers. It is usually equipped with the same kinds of sensory devices that you see on a self-driving car, including LIDAR, cameras, conventional radar, etc. Seems on the surface like it is just like a self-driving car, other than maybe being a bit larger since it has to accommodate a dozen or so passengers. They are often shaped rather tall to allow passengers to get in and out without having to stoop.

What is the difference then between the self-driving shuttles and the AI self-driving cars? It's all about where they drive, how they drive, and the "thinking" or AI involved in the driving. These self-driving shuttles are usually confined to a designated geographical area. They are zoned into a geo-fence, which limits where they can go. This is important because it keeps them in driving areas that are well-known and constrained. A true AI self-driving car can go anywhere, and does not need to be limited to a particular geographical area. The shuttles are kept in a cage.

Furthermore, the cage is mapped and mapped again. The shuttle "knows" entirely the routes and what the roadways consist of. In the case of AI self-driving cars, a Level 5 (topmost capability) self-driving car must be able to handle new roads and new routes, and be able to figure out what to do on-the-fly. For the shuttles, it's almost entirely pre-canned. There isn't much computational effort involved in terms of gauging what the road ahead might be and how to navigate it. Even though you can't see any apparent rails, think of the shuttles like trains on rails, and a train just moves ahead on a pre-determinate path. That's what the shuttles do.

Speed is another important difference. The shuttles usually go about 5 to 10 mph, moving along at a slow pace. This is helpful to the shuttles since they have time to use their sensors to figure out whether a guest has stepped into the roadway and thus come to a halt. Halting is pretty easy at that speed. Though the shuttles can usually go faster such as 20 to 30 mph, doing so is risky. The stopping time is longer and so less safe. Plus, stopping at that speed will likely toss around the guests that are riding in the shuttle. And the sensory data needs to be processed much more quickly.

A true AI self-driving car is expected to zoom along at freeway speeds of 70 to 80 mph. The sensory data needs to be rapidly obtained and processed. Decisions about driving by the AI needs to occur extremely rapidly. Actions taken will need to take into account the long stopping times and the dangers of swerving or turning upside down the car. I think we all instinctively know that going 5 mph versus 80 mph is a big, big, big difference. For those of you that have teenagers that drive, you probably started them in a parking lot where they drove at 5 mph, and you dreaded the fact that soon they would be on regular roads at 20 mph and then eventually on freeways at 80 mph. The difference of driving skills and the time that you have to make decisions and react is like the difference between night and day between those slow speeds and the faster speeds.

I think you can see why I say that the self-driving shuttles aren't Jack Kennedy. They are kept in a geographical cage, the cage is well mapped beforehand, they tend to take the same routes over and over, they move at slow speeds, they can stop readily easily, and they don't need to do much in terms of cognitive types of skills. Self-driving cars need to be able to navigate all kinds of roads and routes, they are not constrained within a geo-fence, and they need to be able to have cognitive skills equivalent to humans in order to properly drive the vehicle.

This is not to say that Disney is somehow mistaken by going ahead with the self-driving shuttles. I think it makes a lot of sense. I am just saying that the reporters that then declare that we have arrived at the era of self-driving vehicles will be mistaken and will be providing "fake news" (see Chapter 10 about AI fake news). Over and again, we'll likely see gushing stories by reporters that are wide-eyed and excited to see the future has arrived. Look, they'll say, proof positive that self-driving vehicles are ready for the roads. I am sure that Disney will allow reporters to go on the shuttles when first trials have occurred, and those reporters will dutifully file stories about the wonderment of the shuttles.

In that sense, it will be "good" because it will add more fuel to the energy and drive toward true self-driving cars. The stocks of firms that make self-driving cars will get a boost, since the feel-good stories about the self-driving shuttles will spread over to the self-driving cars arena. Very few will realize that these are night and day differences. All they will know is that a vehicle with four wheels and transporting passengers seemed to be able to work and do so without incident. Voila, self-driving cars must be good too.

There is a dual-edged sword to this. Suppose that a Disney self-driving shuttle gets into an accident. Yikes! This could drive down the stocks of self-driving car makers. If Disney cannot make it work, who can? Some pundits will step forward and point out that Disney is not a Google, it is not an Uber, it is not a Ford. How could one expect a company that makes themes parks and fun family-friendly movies to also be at the forefront of self-driving vehicles?

Anyway, as you can see, the advent of self-driving shuttles such as those that are possibly coming to Disney will be a means for the public and regulators to get a taste of self-driving vehicles. It won't be the same as self-driving cars and it won't be using as sophisticated AI, but at least it will be using the rudiments and allow for further progress in the direction of true self-driving cars. The self-driving shuttle companies realize they need to continually up their game, and that they cannot allow their shuttles to remain in the brainless category for very long. Once self-driving cars get good, the expectations for the self-driving shuttles will rise too.

You might be aware of the children's story about the little train that could, which involves a train that keeps saying "I think I can" as it tries to proceed ahead. The self-driving shuttles, even as brainless and robotic as they might be at day one, are like those trains that are striving to someday be thinkers. Making and selling them today for highly constrained circumstances is handy and a money maker as society warms up to the self-driving future. People might not know that they are not yet in the future when they ride on one of those shuttles, but at the same time they are supporting ultimately a future involving self-driving cars. Those brainless shuttles will someday get their brains. Don't be surprised if you get onto one of those shuttles and hear the song from the Wizard of Oz about if it only had a brain. It will soon enough.

CHAPTER 9

FIRST SALVO
IN CLASS ACTION LAWSUITS
FOR DEFECTIVE
SELF-DRIVING CARS

CHAPTER 9

FIRST SALVO
IN CLASS ACTION LAWSUITS
FOR DEFECTIVE SELF-DRIVING CARS

Cars, can't live without them, can't live with them (if there are onerous defects).

As an expert witness in court cases involving computer systems, and formerly an Arbitrator for the American Arbitration Association on their Computer Disputes panel, I want to take you into the world of computer related lawsuits as they emerge in the AI and self-driving realm. Get ready for quite a ride. We'll start by considering major class action lawsuits in the automotive realm, beginning with some whoppers that were not about computers but instead involved various kinds of automobile equipment and car design related defects. This lays a handy foundation for the newly emerging lawsuits that involve AI in cars.

Do you remember the famous case of the Ford Motor Company scandal over the Pinto cars that seemed to ignite on fire when struck at the back of the car where the gas tank was mounted? That was in the 1970s and eventually involved a class action lawsuit, during which it was revealed that Ford knew about the problem but opted to do nothing since it was calculated to be cheaper to pay out claims rather than get the problem fixed. Executives eventually were criminally indicated for negligent homicide. It was a huge story for several years. Today, mentioning "Pinto" invokes a kind of keyword or implied suggestion that you are referring to a potentially severe defect and can be applied to any kind of product. Watch out for that washing machine, it's a Pinto – which some reporters exclaimed when last year there was the case of a brand of washing machine that went a kilter and the internal spinning parts flew apart during normal use.

If you weren't around in the 1970s and haven't ever heard about the Ford Pinto, I offer the case of the Ford Explorer SUV that was prone to rollovers in the year 2000. At first, critics said that it was the overall design of the SUV that made it defective. Presumably, the car was slightly lopsided by its design and so upon particular driving maneuvers it was easily topple over. Imagine when you try to balance an object on its edge and there is too much weight toward one side or the other. The National Highway Traffic Safety Administration investigated and they said it was the tires. Firestone made the tires and all of sudden they had the bright light of accusatory defects on them. It was a mess and class action lawsuits were involved.

One more famous case that's even more recent involves the Toyota Lexus scandal in 2009. Some people died when the Lexus would occasionally seemingly go out-of-control. Initially, Toyota claimed that the root cause was the floor mats. Their theory was that the floor mat would inch up toward the floor pedals and jam-up the braking and accelerator pedals from aptly being able to work. Doubts were cast on this theory. Ultimately, during the class action lawsuit, Toyota admitted that it might also be that there was a defective problem with the accelerator pedal. At times, the "sticky pedal" would remain affixed in a given depressed level and was not readily budged by the human driver. In 2014, Toyota paid a $1.2 billion dollar fine and admitted that they had misled consumers, they had concealed the problem, and they had made deceptive statements about what they knew and what the problem was.

Why this history lesson about cars, defects, and class action lawsuits? Because we are now entering into the age of self-driving car defects, along with the equally ubiquitous class action lawsuits to go along with the matter. Indeed, recently the first such salvo was launched when a class action lawsuit against Tesla was filed.

Let the battle begin. There are some very hungry class action lawyers that would love to get some dough out of the bonanza of self-driving cars by going after the self-driving car makers. The bigger the car maker, the juicer the target. I am guessing that class action lawsuit attorneys have a dartboard setup in their offices and that the name of each of the self-driving car makers are shown at various positions on the board. At the center of the target board are the biggest auto makers. It's like the old joke about why the bank robber robs banks, and the answer is because that's where the money is. Going after startups that are making self-driving cars is not very smart and nor lucrative. The anticipation by these cagey lawyers of the big auto makers rolling out self-driving cars is like a tiger ready to pounce on its prey. Tesla right now is the best such target because it has the most self-driving car related vehicles in the hands of consumers, and they are rich enough as a company to make it worthwhile to go for the big bucks out of them.

I would like to add that this is much more than just ambulance chasing. We definitely have self-driving car makers that are not taking safety seriously (as I have emphasized in numerous of my pieces on AI and self-driving cars). I have repeatedly exhorted the self-driving car makers to put due attention toward safety. Most are still not listening. Most are blindly pushing ahead with the "fundamentals" of getting the AI to simply drive a car, and aren't as worried about safety issues. A lot of the software developers are also of the types that think of safety as an after-thought. For them, until a self-driving car demonstrably exhibits safety issues and actually harms or kills, only then will the light bulb come on that maybe they should devote serious attention to safety.

Let's take a close look at the class action lawsuit filed against Tesla regarding their self-driving car capabilities. Keep in mind that when I say self-driving car capabilities, there are five defined levels of self-driving cars and that we are still not anywhere near the topmost sophisticated Level 5. Right now, self-driving cars are around Level 3. I mention this because if we are now having class action lawsuits, I can readily predict that once we actually get to Level 5 that we will then have a torrent of such lawsuits. The more the AI on-board, the greater the chances of defects and defective actions by the self-driving car.

In this first salvo, the lawsuit claims that Tesla provided a nonfunctional Enhanced Autopilot AP2.0 capability. For those of you that aren't devotees of Tesla, you might not be aware that around October 2016 there was an effort by Tesla to provide new features for their Autopilot that they referred to as AP2.0. It cost around $10,000 and was said to include 8 surround cameras, 12 ultrasonic sensors, and software that would be greatly improved over AP1. AP2 was supposed to provide or enhance the active cruise control, lane holding, collision warning, automatic emergency braking, and other nifty features. These are often referred to as Enhanced Autopilot (EAP) and Full Self-Driving (FSD).

These were marketed by Tesla, as easily proven by looking at their ads plastered on billboards and web sites. What the class action lawsuit claims is that:

1. Many of these features were delivered later than promised,
2. Many of these features have never been provided,
3. Many of the provided features do not do what was promised,
4. Many of the provided feature are defective.

The first two claims, namely that Tesla was late in providing a feature or that it has not yet provided a promised feature, those are more so claims about the potential misleading of consumers. This involves showing that Tesla promised something and should be dinged because the consumer didn't get it when promised or has never received it. The marketplace has often let innovators get away with this kind of thing, and we've seen firms like Apple that had made promises for new technology and then didn't quite deliver on-time. This is bad, certainly, but not as bad in a sense as perhaps the other two claims. Not getting something that you paid for is bad, yes, but as you'll see in a moment, getting something that you paid for and if it is not working right, or worse if it works wrong, that's the real hot water.

Allow me to emphasize that I am not letting Tesla or any self-driving car maker off-the-hook if they make a promise for delivering features and do not do so. It's a typical dirty trick to try and convince consumers to wait and buy their product, creating doubt about getting a competing product that does not have those features. I think such hollow promises do need to be kept, and that anyone making such promises needs to pay the penalty for false promises.

I also don't ascribe to the viewpoint that "they are innovators and so we can't complain when they are unable to deliver on new innovations" kind of mindset. Many that are beloved Tesla buyers say that they aren't upset when Tesla makes a promise and delivers late, since they are so devoted that they are willing to overlook such a guffaw. Genius takes time, they will offer defensively. I say hogwash. Promise, and keep to your promise. If you can't accurately predict when you are going to deliver then you have no business making a promise, and else you must be accountable to what you pledged.

In terms of the other two claims, notably that the provided features don't work as promised and that in some instances are defective, these are quite serious since it can make a life-or-death difference for those using the Tesla cars that have AP2.0.

Here's some of the accusations:

- Essentially unusable
- Demonstrably dangerous
- Erratic
- Buyers became beta-testers
- Half-baked software
- Behaves as if a drunk driver is at the wheel
- Not effectively designed
- Not safe
- Not "stress-free"

These are obviously quite serious accusations. The assertion that some of the features are erratic and demonstrably dangerous are clearly of great concern. Engaging the Autopilot would presumably be done under the assumption that the capability is well-tested and works properly and safely. The lawsuit points out that Tesla had even promised that using the Autopilot AP2.0 would make driving "stress-free," which is a bit of marketing hyperbole and we'll have to see whether the court considers it as a true promise or something weaker and less binding. I might tell you that the new tires on your car will make your driving stress-free, and the question arises as to whether that's an outright promise or not, and what it means to be stress-free (can we ever be truly stress-free, a philosopher might ask?).

The suggestion that the AP2.0 drives like a drunk driver is especially interesting. In Chapter 22, I debunk the notion that by adopting self-driving cars that we'll reduce to zero any car related deaths due to drunk driving. I have pointed out that though we might reduce the human drunk drivers, we are still faced with AI that might have flaws, errors, bugs, or omissions that cause it to sometimes be as lousy a driver as a drunk driver. I guess these lawyers must be reading my pieces!

Like any class action lawsuit, the legal action is intended to cover those consumers that would have been potentially impacted by the claims. In this case, the lawsuit seeks to encompass any Tesla buyer that within the designated time frame had either bought or leased certain models of the Tesla car brand. Sought are the economic losses to those Tesla impacted owners due to the alleged false promises. What makes this claim a bit less biting is that there aren't actually Tesla owners that were directly injured or died due to these alleged false promises. I mention this because it is much easier to get a win if you have some visceral and dramatic actual injury damage that has occurred, rather than just trying to show that a promise was broken and that somehow the car owners were less safe or more stressed.

Imagine if there were Pinto cars that had not at first exploded or caught on fire, and if someone had figured out beforehand that there was a potential for danger and death due to the design. Launching a class action lawsuit to say that there is the potential for a Pinto to be a killer is one thing, but doing so after there have been actual cases is another. Courts seeing pictures of burning Pintos and grieving family and relatives makes for a more compelling case.

Whenever you file these kinds of class action lawsuits, you have to have someone specifically that was considered to be impacted by the claim and they must be explicitly named in the lawsuit. You can't just file in general and say that someone somewhere might be impacted. The named claimants then are shown to be specific examples and then you make the case that anyone else can be logically considered equally so impacted. In this case, there are 3 named plaintiffs, each of which allegedly bought the in-scope Tesla, and it says they paid anywhere from $81,000 to $113,000 for the cars.

Usually, the named plaintiffs aren't going to get incredibly enriched by these cases, which we think of as being true because of wild cases like having hot coffee spilled on you are at your local fast food chain. Mainly what happens is the plaintiffs get something, the members of the class get something, and usually the lawyer get a hefty payout. I know it easy to be cynical and say that these lawsuits are only about the lawyers getting rich. The other side of the coin involves the aspect that the lawyers usually take these cases without any upfront promise of getting paid, and so they are at risk of making nothing on the case, which could require tons and tons of work on their part. Also, one could say that they are "crusaders" in that they force companies to relook at what they do and can therefore have a positive impact on getting car makers to be more serious about safety. That being said, I was not pressured into saying this by any of the attorneys that I know, and I am merely trying to point out that there are ambulance chasers and there are also do-gooders. You decide what's the circumstance in this instance.

What is especially alarming in this Tesla case involves some anecdotes that were included in the filing. Such anecdotes need to be taken with a grain of salt since they were apparently plucked from the Internet (see my piece on AI self-driving fake news). Anyway, one anecdote said that their Tesla with AP2.0 supposedly was going 50 mph and the radar spotted a bridge ahead, which then caused the Autopilot to slam on the brakes. This goes back to my other exhortations here about how we need to be mindful that the sensors of self-driving cars can produce false readings, and that the AI software might also take even true sensory data and falsely make mistakes about interpreting it or taking inappropriate actions. This goes to the issue of making the AI software more robust and having safety controls all throughout it.

The attorneys for the lawsuit are asserting that Tesla marketed proverbial smoke-and-mirrors to consumers. Fortunately, so far, no one seems to have yet been physically injured or died due to the claimed smoke-and-mirrors, though in a sense this is "unfortunate" for purposes of this legal case. It is unfortunate for the legal case because it will be harder to show actual damages. It is also unfortunate because Tesla may or may not take the case as seriously otherwise. And it is also unfortunate because the other self-driving car makers might also take it as less serious matter. Indeed, some of the auto-makers might simply tone down their marketing claims. This is helpful, but if they are still in the backroom churning out flawed AI software for their self-driving cars, then they are only dealing with solving the appearances rather than the substance of the problem.

As I have previously noted about Tesla, the darling of the industry automaker dodged a bullet with the case last year involving the human driver that had the Autopilot on and he ran into a truck, killing him, which the federal investigation put the blame on the human driver (since, in theory, Tesla continues to say that it is the human driver that must be aware at all times and holds the final responsibility for the driving of the car). We'll need to see whether this newly filed lawsuit can actually qualify for a class action (it has to show proof of class nature), and see whether the claims can be proven in court. Tesla might settle in some fashion beforehand, especially if it wants to avoid having to air any potential dirty laundry, plus if it wants to possibly avoid a public relations backlash during the lawsuit.

For me, I want this case to hopefully be a wake-up call for the AI community and those AI developers participating in the grand experiment of creating self-driving cars. It is exciting to think that in our generation we will have self-driving cars, and somehow achieve a Jetson-like accomplishment akin to everyone having jet packs. AI developers need to take this desire to be first with self-driving capabilities as also a responsibility to make them safe. I realize that for those of you software engineers tolling away at a self-driving car maker that you might say that upper management doesn't care about the safety and you are under pressure to churn out the other code. Not sure if that's going to be a valid excuse down-the-road, once that self-driving car you helped code injures or kills. You might be faced with civil legal action, criminal legal action, and your own sense of humanity and whether you did what you could and did the right thing. AI and self-driving cars are fun, but also involve life-and-death.

CHAPTER 10

AI FAKE NEWS

ABOUT

SELF-DRIVING CARS

CHAPTER 10

AI FAKE NEWS
ABOUT SELF-DRIVING CARS

Fake news.

That's an expression that has gained a lot of notoriety lately. One person's fake news often seems to be another person's real news. Real news versus fake news. Fake news versus real news. How can we discern one from the other? Believe it or not, some states like California are now even trying to make mandatory a core course for all high school students that would involve teaching them the differences between fake news and real news. Though this generally seems like a good idea, questions abound about what constitutes fake news versus real news. Also, some worry that this would become nothing more than an agenda to try and impose upon impressionable minds a particular political bent, whether liberal or conservative, and use the guise of outing fake news as a means to brainwash our children.

For now, I'd like to concentrate on a specific genre of fake news. There is a lot of "fake news" about AI and self-driving cars. I see it every day in the headlines of major media outlets. It appears on the back-page stories and the front-page stories. It creeps into the dialogue about self-driving cars. The general public is misled by many of these stories. Regulators are being misled. Companies are both helping to mislead and also being misled. The bonanza of self-driving cars has produced a jackpot of fake news. I'll explain what I mean by fake news, and you can decide whether my perspective of fake news is your perspective too, or whether you consider my fake news to be real news. You decide.

One place to start when talking about fake news is to initially aim at hoaxes or scams. I think that we can all pretty much agree that if a news story is based on a hoax or scam, we would likely be willing to label that news as fake news. Let's suppose I reported that John Smith has turned lead into gold. This is of course the infamous alchemists dream. Mankind has sought to turn various ores into gold as long as gold has been considered a valuable commodity. If I take John Smith's word that he did turn lead into gold, and I don't do any background research, and if he really did not turn lead into gold, some would say that this was fake news. He didn't actually turn lead into gold. It's a fake.

Suppose that I did some background research and had found out that it is possible to actually turn lead into gold, in spite of the assumption that it would seem an impossible task. Via nuclear transmutation, involving converting a chemical element from one kind into another, presumably we could turn lead into gold. If John Smith is a renowned chemist at a top-notch university, and I take his word that he turned lead into gold, would my news reporting still be considered fake news? Well, if he didn't actually turn lead into gold, and if that's what the claim was, it seems that it is still fake news, even though the possibility of it happening was reasonable. This just means I didn't do much a reporting job to ferret out whether the news was true or fake.

How does this apply to AI and self-driving cars? Let's take an example that I previously wrote about, involving the self-driving truck that in Colorado delivered a bunch of beer (see my article on self-driving trucks and cars).

Here's some headlines that heralded the feat:

- "Driverless beer run: Bud makes shipment with self-driving truck" as per CNBC

- "Uber's self-driving truck makes its first commercial delivery: Beer" as per Los Angeles Times

- "Self-driving truck makes first trip: 120-mile beer run" as per USA Today

- "Uber's Otto debuts delivery by self-driving truck" as per Wall Street Journal

Are these headlines appropriate for what actually took place? As mentioned in my earlier piece on this matter, I pointed out that the self-driving truck only did the freeway portion of the ride and did not do the actual pick-up and delivery on side streets, it was guarded by highway patrol while it did the self-driving, it had done the same route several times before to train on it, the route had been cleared of basically any traffic or obstacles, and so on.

The average reader would likely assume from the headlines that self-driving trucks actually exist and are good enough to make pick-ups and deliveries, all by themselves. Going beyond the headlines, the articles barely mentioned the numerous caveats and limitations of the feat. Turns out that this was a huge public relations boost for Uber and Otto, while the mainstream media played a part in aiding the PR stunt. The media liked the story since it was a feel-good kind of story and sold newspapers and content. Reporters didn't need to dig very far into the story because it was seen as a light oriented story, one that presumably doesn't need the same level of scrutiny as say a story about a cure for cancer.

You can say that the feat did happen and so in that sense it is not like my suggestion of someone falsely claiming that they could turn lead into gold. At the same time, I would argue that the self-driving truck story suggests that lead was turned into gold, and the mainstream media got it wrong by assuming this to be true. There was a taint of fake news that got past most of the mainstream media filters. Many stories about AI are often relished by the mainstream media. They want to run headlines and do stories about the exciting future of AI. There is also the other side of that coin, namely they like to also run headlines that AI will bring us humans utter destruction and AI will take over the world.

Here's a headline that seems reasonable: "Ready or Not, Driverless Cars Are Coming" as per Time magazine.

The headline doesn't say that driverless cars are here, and so buys itself some latitude by simply asserting that one day we will see driverless cars. Admittedly that's pretty hard to debate since yes, some day we will have truly driverless cars. Suppose I told you that the headline for that Times magazine piece came from the year 2014. The article is still Okay since it never stated when we would have driverless cars, but the implication in the headline and the piece was that we were on the verge of seeing driverless cars. We aren't there yet, and it is now some three years after that article was published.

This also brings up the notion of what it means when you use the wording of a driverless car. I've discussed at length the nuances of self-driving car versus autonomous and driverless cars (see my article on this topic). In any case, the Time magazine piece could be considered correct if you consider the Tesla to be a driverless car. I don't think any reasonable person considers Tesla to be a driverless car, and indeed even Tesla emphasizes that it is a car that must be human-ready to be driven at all times, regardless of whether the Autopilot is engaged.

As mentioned, the news does not also paint a necessarily positive picture about AI and self-driving cars.

Here's a headline that caught my eye: "Does AI Make Self-Driving Cars Less Safe?" This piece causes anyone that is truly into AI to wonder what they are trying to assert. Turns out that the piece claims that machine learning is too limited and will make self-driving cars more dangerous than otherwise. An expert is quoted about this.

Well, let's unpack that logic. If we only use machine learning, and limit it to the nature of what we understand machine learning to be today, and if that is what we are going to label as AI, perhaps the story makes sense. I've written that machine learning of today can get us into some bad spots. Suppose a machine learning technique causes a self-driving car to "learn" that it is okay to try and go over a curb to make a right turn at a red light. This could end-up being a catastrophic tactic that ultimately would kill either the passengers or pedestrians. Machine learning that is unbounded and unrestrained is indeed questionable. It is for those reasons that the rest of the AI has to help to guide and bound the machine learning. Likewise, the human developers that put in place machine learning for self-driving cars need to do so with the appropriate kinds of restrictions and safety measures.

Here's a provocative headline that appeared in the prestigious MIT Technology Review: "Why Self-Driving Cars Must Be Programmed to Kill." You've got to give the editor and writer some credit for coming up with a catchy headline. Similar to my piece about the ethics of self-driving cars, the MIT Technology Review article discusses that ultimately a self-driving car will need to make some tough decisions about who to kill. If a self-driving car is going down a street and a child suddenly darts into the road, should the self-driving car take evasive action that might cause the car to swerve off-the-road into a telephone pole that possibly kills the passengers and saves the child, or should the self-driving car "decide" to plow into and kill the child but save the car passengers. That's the rub of the matter and the MIT Technology Review article covers the same type of ethical dilemmas that self-driving cars and car makers must address.

Take a look at this bold and assertive headline: "Humans vs robots: Driverless cars are safer than human driven vehicles." What do you think of the claim made in this headline? We've seen many such claims being made that self-driving cars are going to save the world and eliminate car related deaths. I've debunked this notion in my piece on the goal of zero car fatalities having a zero chance of happening. This particular headline takes a more nuanced approach and tries to suggest that self-driving cars are safer drivers than human drivers. This is something we cannot prove to be the case, and so the headline is at least misleading. Our logic tells us that if we eliminate all emotion and have an always aware robotic driver that presumably it must be safer than a human driver that is susceptible to normal human foibles.

But this also omits the aspect that humans have abilities that we don't know whether we will ever be able to have embodied in a self-driving car. For example, consider the role of common sense. When you as a human are driving a car, you are aware of the significance of the world around the car. You understand that physics plays a role in what the car can and cannot do. You know that pedestrians that look toward you might be subtly signaling to you that they are going to dash out into the street. You might see a child playing ball up ahead in the front yard of a house and assume that the child might wander into the street to get their ball. These are aspects that we are still not expecting that the upcoming self-driving cars will be able to do.

Someday, maybe years and years into the future, we might have self-driving cars that have this same kind of human based common sense. So, we might suggest that self-driving cars in one hundred years will be safer than human drivers, but it is harder to make such a claim in the nearer term. We also need to consider what it means to say that someone or something is safer. Is that measured by the least number of deaths derived by being a driver? Or by least number of injuries? Or least number of accidents involved in?

The suggestion that self-driving cars are going to eliminate car related deaths is a popular one in the mainstream media. This brings us to another aspect of fake news, namely the echo chamber effect.

Often, fake news gains traction by the aspect that others pick-up the fake news and repeat it. This continues over and over. Furthermore, other news that might counter the fake news tends to be filtered out. These are called filter bubbles. There are lots of stakeholders that want and hope that self-driving cars will materially reduce car related deaths, and I also certainly wish the same to be true. The thing about this is that we should not believe this assertion simply because it keeps getting repeated.

The general hubbub and excitement over self-driving cars is going to continue and we'll have "fake news" (or at least misleading news) that will continue to support the surge toward self-driving cars. Without this push, we might not be able to make as much progress as we've been able to do. A few years ago, no one was willing to put big bucks into self-driving cars and the field of autonomous vehicles barely survived off of federal grants and other charitable kinds of support. All of the dollars flowing into self-driving cars is exciting and aiding the progress that otherwise would have only happened in sporadic bits and spurts.

Some real news that might come eventually as a shocker could be an appalling accident by a self-driving car. I've written about the Tesla incident involving the autopilot-engaged Tesla that rammed into a truck and killed the driver of the Tesla. This was cleared by the feds by saying that the automation was not at fault due to the human driver ultimately being responsible for the driving of the car. That's a perspective that luckily saved Tesla and the self-driving car industry, though would seem of little solace to the driver that died and his family.

Remember when the oil tanker Exxon Valdez went aground in Prince William Sound, spilling many millions of gallons of oil and creating an environmental nightmare? That took place in 1989. Or, do you remember the 1985 crash of the Delta Airline flight that was flying from Florida to Los Angeles and crashed due to riding through a thunderstorm and not being able to detect microbursts? Both of these tragedies led to new regulations and also advances in technology. For the Valdez, we got advances in ship navigation systems and also improved spill detection and spill clean-up technology. For the Delta flight, we got new airborne wind-shear detection systems and improved alert systems that made flying safer for us all.

I am predicting that we will soon have a self-driving car that causes a dreadful accident. The self-driving car will be found at fault, or at least that it contributed to the fault. I shudder to think that this is going to happen. I don't want it to happen. When it does happen, the headlines will suddenly change tone and there will be all sorts of hand wringing about how we let self-driving cars get onto the roads. Regulators will be drilled out of office for having let this occur. New regulations will be demanded. All self-driving car makers will be forced to reexamine their systems and safety approaches. A cleansing of the self-driving car marketplace will occur.

This is not a doom and gloom kind of prediction. It is the likely scenario of a build-up of excitement that will have a bit of a burst bubble. It won't kill off the industry. The industry will continue to exist and grow. What it will do is make the news media more questioning and skeptical. We'll see less stories of the uplifting nature about AI and self-driving cars. And for those self-driving car makers that have invested in sufficient safety systems and capabilities, they will be rewarded while those firms that have given lip service to that aspect of their AI will find themselves in trouble.

Be on the watch for fake news about self-driving cars. Keep your wits about you. Many old timers know and lived through the early AI heydays of the 1980s and 1990s, and then the AI winter arrived. There were naysayers at the time that derided a lot of the AI fake news that was being published (well, it wasn't called fake news then, but it had the same sentiment). We are now in the AI spring and things are looking up. Let's hope that the sun keeps shining and the flowers will bloom.

CHAPTER 11

RANCOROUS RANKING OF SELF-DRIVING CARS

CHAPTER 11

RANCOROUS RANKING
OF SELF-DRIVING CARS

Suppose you were asked to rank the presidents of the United States. Who is your top pick?

Maybe Abraham Lincoln or perhaps George Washington? Those seem like reasonable choices. Popular and known for having accomplished various outstanding acts as president, both Lincoln and Washington would seem like valid selections and consistently appear on the topmost rankings. If you suddenly saw a ranking that listed Jimmy Carter as the top president of all time, what would you think? Surprising, maybe even causing you to raise your eyebrows in partial disbelief. What about if a ranking indicated that William Henry Harrison was the topmost ranked president of all time? Shocking, perhaps? Most Americans don't even recognize Harrison's name as having been a president at all and would be puzzled that Harrison made it to the top of any ranking.

A ranking can be established in whatever manner desired. When I asked just now for your top pick of presidents, you probably assumed that I meant "top" as based on maybe popularity or notable accomplishments. I could have been using some other criteria. If I were ranking them by shortest time served in the presidential office, William Henry Harrison would come out at the top of the list because he only served for 31 days as president. I could have ranked the presidents by their height, in which case Lincoln happens to be the topmost of the ranking due to his have been six feet plus in height, and would be followed closely by Lyndon Johnson.

Using just one criteria for a ranking is a commonly preferred method, especially since it is easy to comprehend and simple to do the ranking. Unfortunately, one criterium alone often does not tell the whole story and provides a misleading ranking. For example, ranking the presidents by their length of time in office or by their height is not very illuminating per se. So, rankings will shift toward multiple criteria, such as for a president it might be attributes of their economic achievements while in office, and their administrative skills, their relations with Congress during their presidency, and so on.

Why all this focus on presidential rankings? I just wanted to get you ready for a recent ranking of self-driving car makers and prepare you to be somewhat shocked, but also ready for the surprising rank order. The moment you hear or see a ranking of self-driving car makers, I hope that you'll be of a mind to question how the ranking was undertaken. Was it done with one criteria or more than one? How were the criteria chosen? Were the criteria appropriate for doing a ranking? Etc.

Here's a recent ranking of Top 10 self-driving car makers (as derived by a research company called Navigant Research, shown above):

1. Ford
2. GM
3. Renault-Nissan Alliance
4. Daimler
5. Volkswagen Group
6. BMW
7. Google Waymo (tied with Volvo et al)
8. Volvo/Autoliv/Zenuity (tied with Google Waymo)
9. Delphi
10. Hyundai Motor Group

Take a close look at the Top 10 ranking.

Where is Google Waymo on the ranking? At seventh position (oddly enough; plus also tied with Volvo at 7th), far below firms such as Ford, GM, and others. Given that Google Waymo has been pursuing self-driving car technology for many years, and that it is considered a bold and vested developer of self-driving capabilities, it is a bellwether of AI advances, and has by far the most miles logged of self-driving cars (2 million or more miles), it is a bit shocking to see it listed toward the bottom of the Top 10 ranking. In fact, it would be shocking to see it toward the bottom of any Top 10 ranking about self-driving cars, no matter what criteria you might reasonably choose.

Take another even closer look at the Top 10 ranking. Tell me where Tesla sits on the ranking. Don't see it. Yes, that's right, it is not even listed in the Top 10. They placed Tesla outside the Top 10, noting Tesla as being in 12th position. Meanwhile, in the news, there has been a recent rise in Tesla stock and led it to become the most valuable U.S. automaker. Ford, which is ranked at the top of this Top 10 list, now has been surpassed in market value by Tesla, which of course this ranking didn't even put Tesla into the Top 10 at all.

Admittedly, as a car maker overall, regardless of self-driving cars, Ford last year made $4.6 billion and produced 6.7 million vehicles, while Tesla lost $675 million last year and sold about 77,000 cars. By those statistics, it does seem odd that Tesla would have a larger market share than Ford. The marketplace is reacting not solely to the numbers of how each firm performs, but also to what the firm represents for the future. Right or wrong, the marketplace perceives the Tesla as being worth more than Ford. Surveys suggest that it is because Tesla is perceived as nimble, futuristic, and breaking outside the boundaries of conventional car makers. Ford tends to be perceived as stodgy, stuck in old ways, and unlikely to be able to adjust to changing times.

Let's get back to the self-driving car ranking. Why did the research company place Ford at the top of the list, and put Google Waymo in seventh place, and not even put Tesla into the Top 10? Notably too, Uber is not on the list either (it was ranked in 16th place).

According to the research firm, these are the criteria they used to do the ranking:
1. Vision
2. Go-to market strategy
3. Partners
4. Production strategy
5. Technology
6. Sales, marketing and distribution
7. Product capability
8. Product quality and reliability
9. Product portfolio
10. Staying power

They claim to have used a proprietary methodology to weigh and combine those criteria, so we don't really know whether any particular criteria got more or less of a punch in doing this ranking.

In terms of Tesla, they reported that it is worrisome whether Tesla has staying power (criteria #10), given that it keeps losing money and might eventually fold. This certainly is a valid reason to be skeptical of Tesla's long-term viability, and especially as a self-driving car maker it might fall apart entirely as an automotive company, regardless of how well it advances self-driving cars. The research firm also questioned Elon Musk's insistence that LIDAR is not needed for achieving self-driving cars (see my piece on LIDAR for my remarks on this topic). Some believe that LIDAR is the only way to arrive at true self-driving cars (presumably encompassed by their criteria #5), and so the longer that Tesla avoids using LIDAR the further it will ultimately fall behind in terms of getting toward a true Level-5 self-driving car, some assert.

The explanation about Tesla almost makes sense as to why Tesla is not ranked highly, but it still is a shocker to think that it doesn't make even the Top 10. Several of the companies listed in the positions of 5 through 10 are not especially far along on self-driving cars, and are little known in the self-driving car marketplace. Those car makers are certainly known for making cars, and have histories to support their earnest commitment to the automotive industry, but it still catches one's throat to think of them as higher in self-driving cars than Tesla.

What about Uber? Uber has been beleaguered lately of all sorts of company crises and seems to be digging a hole on public perception. It also continues to lose money. According to the research firm, Uber is a duck out of water in that though it has a great ride hailing app, it has no automotive background and experience, it lacks entirely any manufacturing capacity for cars, and it doesn't even sell and market cars. Most analysts are worried that Uber will get caught with a massive fleet of human drivers and become outdated once self-driving cars emerge. Uber itself recognizes this potential danger, and in a recent lawsuit that it is fighting, Uber said in court that the ability to pursue the development of self-driving cars is key to the future viability of the firm (see my piece about self-driving car lawsuits).

Another blow against Uber was the instance of the Uber self-driving car in San Francisco that ran a red light (see my piece about self-driving car accidents). Though none of the self-driving car makers are necessarily perfect right now in terms of their on-the-road experimentation, Uber got a bad roll of the dice on getting caught on video with their Uber car doing something foul. Other self-driving cars have had similar kinds of situations, but so far haven't had the bad luck of getting caught on video and becoming a national and international slur on self-driving cars.

The lowly rankings for Tesla and Uber appear to be logical and understandable, once you dig into the details. The ranking of Google Waymo is harder to grasp. Ranking Google Waymo as seventh place is like putting the most winning horse to-date going into the Kentucky Derby race as being toward the bottom of the pack. According to the research firm, they ranked Google's efforts low because they are not a car maker. Well, yes, that's kind of obvious, and I think we all know that Google is not a car maker. They have tremendous technology and are an innovator. I doubt that anyone has envisioned Google suddenly deciding to start making cars. Instead, we would expect that Google will license or sell their technology, and get into bed with someone else to make self-driving cars that employ Google's tech.

Indeed, we are likely to see each car maker making deals with self-driving car innovators. For example, Ford put $150 million with Baidu for investing in Velodyne, a prominent maker of LIDAR. Ford has put $1 billion into self-driving tech firm Argo AI, a startup. Ford has taken a position in Civil Maps, a 3D mapping company. And so on. No one company is going to win the entire self-driving car race. We are going to end-up with lots of interrelated companies all intersecting with each other. We are also going to have lots of promises about when self-driving cars are going to be on-the-road, such as Ford's CEO claiming that they will roll-out a Level-4 car by the year 2021.

Besides having numerous partnerships, alliances, licensing deals, and the like, we are also going to see added players come into the mix.

Insiders of the self-driving car industry know that Apple has been toying with being in the self-driving car space. Recently, Apple filed a permit with the Department of Motor Vehicles (DMV) in California to carry out testing of self-driving cars on California public roadways. This follows the notable rumors a few months ago that Apple was letting go of many of their self-driving car team members and reassigning them to other projects. At the time, it appeared that Apple was perhaps leaning toward making self-driving cars. Now, some believe that Apple is aiming instead at making the software for self-driving cars, and will cut a deal with a car maker about the making of the cars.

Does it make sense to see Apple involved in self-driving cars? Yes, many assert, it does make a lot of sense. Apple wants to make sure that when you are enjoying your ride in your self-driving car that you are doing so with your iPhone and plugged into the Apple-based entertainment system of your AI based car. They are worried that they might be shutout of the self-driving car bonanza. Self-driving cars will be an ecosystem of interconnected partners, and Apple wants to be on that list.

By the way, Apple wasn't even in the list of 18 firms chosen to be ranked by the research firm. This illustrates how fluid the self-driving car market continues to be. The research firm acknowledged in their report that the market will be changing over the years. We'll see new players pop-in and others drop out. GM, ranked in the #2 position by the research firm, recently pledged to hire over 1,000 workers in California to bolster their efforts toward self-driving cars, boosting their autonomous vehicle division that is located in the Silicon Valley area of California (this was part of a deal GM made with California to get tax credits).

The huge bucks and dramatic changes coming by the advent of self-driving cars is so tremendous that everyone is going to want a piece of the action. Government agencies at the local, state, and federal level want a piece of the action. Car makers for sure want a piece of the action. Technology firms want a piece of the action. Universities and research think tanks want a piece of the action. Don't be surprised if we see some left-field players that suddenly want into the action, such as major banks, major transportation companies, even major retailers that are trying to find a path out of the brick-and-mortar death of conventional retail. Self-driving cars are going to be a gold rush. Any firm that has the money and the interest will be willing and eager to jump into the fray.

Next time you see a ranking of a self-driving car makers, consider what criteria was used to rank the players. In this case, we saw a ranking that caused quite a media stir, giving new hope to the old-time car makers, and putting the darlings of self-driving cars down in the dumps. This shock value helped the research firm to get its fifteen minutes of fame. It also provides an opportunity to go beyond the usual headlines that typically have Google, Tesla, and Uber in the news about self-driving cars. Whether you agree or not with the criteria used in this particular ranking, it is handy to consider what criteria you should be using. Just like ranking presidents, we all have our own preferences and it is important to be skeptical of any ranking and the bias it has adopted by selecting particular criteria. If you are wondering whether I'll tell you my top ranked president, or my top ranked self-driving car company, sorry, for that you'll need to pay me to get my opinion. Remember, it's a gold rush for all.

CHAPTER 12

PRODUCT LIABILITY

FOR SELF-DRIVING CARS

CHAPTER 12

PRODUCT LIABILITY
FOR SELF-DRIVING CARS

There is a lot of glee these days in the halls of self-driving car developers. We are on fire. Everyone is breathlessly awaiting the next iteration of self-driving cars. Demand for self-driving car developers is extremely keen. Training classes on software development for self-driving car systems engineering are packed to the gills. Car makers are excited to tout their concept cars and also make claims about when their next self-driving car version will hit the streets. Money by the venture capital community is flowing to self-driving car startups. Media loves to run stories about the self-driving cars that are on the horizon.

What a wonderful time to be alive!

The lawyers are also gleeful. With all this money flowing into self-driving cars, we've seen fights on the Intellectual Property (IP) frontlines (see Chapter 9 on the topic of IP lawsuits for self-driving cars). The IP stuff is the most obvious target right now for legal wrangling. We've also seen a recent lawsuit against Tesla that their promised capabilities of Autopilot 2.0 were allegedly slipshod and not what was represented. The Tesla lawsuit is going to be a big eye opener for the entire self-driving car marketplace. It will though take probably several years for the lawsuit against Tesla to play out, and so until we see that Tesla somehow takes a big hit if they lose on it, the lawsuit will be nothing more than a small blip on the radar for self-driving car makers.

We are now though entering into a much bigger frontier for lawsuits in the self-driving car arena. Let me give you an example of what's coming up soon. Audi is bringing out their new model of their Audi A8, and it is claimed to have Level 3 self-driving capabilities (see my article on the Richter scale of self-driving car levels). Up until now, we have essentially had Level 2 self-driving capabilities, though some have argued that Tesla's Autopilot is somewhere between Level 2 and Level 3, and some even say it is Level 3 (this is quite debatable).

According to Audi's own press release: "Audi will introduce what's expected to the world's first to-market Level 3 automated driving system with "Traffic Jam Pilot" in the next generation Audi A8. The system will give drivers the option to travel hands-free up to 35 mph, when certain conditions are met prior to enabling this feature — for instance, the vehicle will ensure it is on a limited-access, divided highway."

The debut of the new Audi A8 with so-called Level 3 capability is slated for July 11. Furthermore, it will be featured in the early July released new Spider-man movie, and will showcase that the driver of the car has taken their hands off the wheel, allowing the Audi A8 to drive itself. This blockbuster movie will potentially help push ahead the Audi A8 in the race to bring self-driving cars to the market. Movie goers will presumably rush out to buy the latest Audi A8. And, their expectations of other car makers will continue to rise, wanting to see similar features on their Ford, Nissan, Toyota, and other cars, else they won't buy any new cars from anyone other than Audi.

Lawyers will likely go to see the new Spider-man movie in droves, wanting to witness the first piece of evidence that will be ultimately held against Audi. What do I mean? I am saying that with great guts goes great risks. Audi is setting itself up for what could be the blockbuster bonanza of self-driving lawsuits. They are certainly a big target since they are a big company (owned by the Volkswagon Group, consisting of Audi, Porsche, Volkswagen, Bentley, Bugatti, Lamborghini, SEAT, Skoda). Their deep pockets make them a tremendous target for any attorney that wants to become rich.

I am talking about a hefty product liability lawsuit. Audi is making the brash claim that their Audi A8 is going to be Level 3. Will consumers understand what Level 3 actually entails? Does Audi even understand what Level 3 entails? Can Audi try to squirm out of any claims that consumers that bought the car really comprehended what Level 3 involves and/or what Audi meant by saying level 3? Let's take a close look at this and explore what product liability is all about.

To make a bona fide defective product liability claim, you need to meet one or more of the following criteria (note: I am referring to U.S. law, and so other countries will differ; also, I am not a lawyer and I am not providing legal advice, so this is my disclaimer and you should go get an attorney if you believe you have a product liability claim):

1. Defective manufacturing of the product
2. Defective design of the product
3. Failure to adequately forewarn about proper use

Let's discuss each of these three aspects.

In the case of a defective manufacturing of a product, this is when a product was fouled-up during the manufacturing process. The product might otherwise have been designed correctly for what it is intended to do, and it might have properly forewarned about how to use it, but during the manufacturing there was a screw-up and so the product that you received had a defect. Thus, it was imperfectly made. If the imperfectly made product then got you into trouble, such as if it was a tire for your car and during manufacturing the tire maker messed-up and the tire had an internal rip, and if then that particular tire upon your car exploded while driving it, you'd have a strong case to win a lawsuit against the tire maker.

In the case of a defective design of a product, this is when a product was designed improperly and regardless whether it is manufactured correctly or not, and regardless of whether you were forewarned about the proper use, its design was wrong to start with. In other words, the product is inherently dangerous, even if it were made perfectly. Suppose you buy a pair of sunglasses and it failed to protect your eyes from UV rays, you might well have a case that by design the sunglasses were dangerous. This aspect can be only pushed so far, since if the item is already dangerous in some manner, like say a meat cleaver, you will have a hard time saying that when it cut off your finger that you believe the meat cleaver by design was unreasonably dangerous. The counter-claim is that by-gosh it's a meat cleaver and so it is apparent that the product would be dangerous.

In the case of failure to forewarn, this involves products that in some way are dangerous but the user of the product was not adequately made aware of the danger. The product has to not be so obvious as to its danger, such as again a meat cleaver is pretty apparent that it has inherent dangers – probably not needed to forewarn that you could cut off your fingers, though a product maker is wise to make such warnings anyway. If a product should only be used in certain ways, and the user should exercise care or special precautions, if those precautions aren't called out by the maker than the product user could go after them saying that they (the user) was not aware of the dangers involved.

Now that we've covered the three major aspects of product liability, let's see what it takes to try and have a bona fide product liability claim that some product is defective. First, you have to actually in some way become injured by the product and it must be a contributing factor of that injury. Simply theorizing that you could get hurt is rarely sufficient. You must have actual damages of some kind. And, the damages must be tied to the product. If the damages done to you weren't related to the product, it will be tossed out since you weren't harmed by the product, even if it turns out that the product is truly defective in some manner.

You also must show that you were using the product as intended. A meat cleaver is intended to carve meat. If you decide to start your own juggling act and toss in the air a meat cleaver, and if in so doing it chops off your hand, this really wasn't the intended use of the meat cleaver. We wouldn't likely expect the meat cleaver maker to have forewarned that you should not use the product for purposes of juggling. There are often way too many bad uses of a product to enumerate them all. The focus usually comes back to whatever is the reasonable intended use of the product, as per what a reasonable person would tend to believe it should be used. Of course, whatever the maker of the product says can have a big impact on that aspect. If the maker of the Joe's meat cleaver advertises that their meat cleaver is for cutting meats and for juggling, they have opened the door to a usage that other meat cleaver makers would not be likely as liable for.

Are you comfortable now that you are up-to-speed about the rudiments of product liability? I hope so, because now we'll take a close look at self-driving cars. We'll use Audi as a case study of what might happen to them, and this is applicable to all other self-driving car makers too.

Audi is claiming that the Audi A8 will have a Level 3 capability. In this instance, they are saying that when the car is in heavy traffic, and on an open highway, with a barrier dividing it from opposing traffic, the Level 3 feature can be engaged to drive the car. During which, the human driver can presumably take their focus off the driving task. It has been reported that the Audi might even have an ability to let the user read their emails or watch a video on the dashboard display. At the same time, it is indicated by Audi in their press release that "Driver Availability Detection confirms that the driver is active and available to intervene. If not, it will bring the car to a safe stop. The vehicle ensures that the road is suitable for piloted driving by detecting features of the surroundings like lane markings, shoulders, and side barriers."

Let's now revisit our three criteria, namely whether a product is defective in its manufacture, whether it is defective in its design, or whether it is defective in forewarning the product user.

One problem for Audi will be whether the car when made actually has no problems in terms of the sensors that contribute to the capability of detecting the surroundings of the car. Any manufacturing defects in that will come to haunt them if someone while using the Level 3 feature gets injured in a car accident. Likewise, if the AI software that carries out the Level 3 has any inherent manufacturing issues (suppose there are bugs in the software), they are looking at a potential product liability claim if someone is injured as a result of that bad manufacturing. And so on for any of the hardware and software components that comprise the Level 3 feature.

Or, it could be that the design itself is flawed. The aspect that they are going to try and ascertain that the driver is still attentive might be so insufficient and weak that it is unable to adequately detect that the user is not paying attention to the road. Or, as I have stated many times in many venues, suppose that the system does not allow sufficient time to alert the human driver to intervene. If the human driver gets just a split second to react to something that has gone beyond the Level 3 capability, and if in so notifying the human driver belatedly that then the car gets into an accident and the driver or passengers are injured, you could claim that the design of the Level 3 was defective.

In terms of the failure to forewarn, I am guessing that the Audi A8 manuals that come with the car will probably try to warn the driver about being careful and mindful when using the Level 3 feature. But, how much of an emphasis there will be could undermine Audi if it is some kind of watered down cautionary explanation. Furthermore, if the manual is not readily available to the driver, such as it is stored in a glovebox and there's no expectation of it being read, this also opens up Audi. You can also bet that the dealerships selling these cars are going to hype the Level 3 feature. As such, I would guess that the buyer of the car will think it does more than what Audi as a manufacturer believes, but that the dealers will be making bolder claims. Likewise, the advertising for the car will further bolster the suggestion that the car maker has not sufficiently forewarned about the limits of the Level 3.

I already am in disagreement about the claims that some have been making about the Audi, namely it seems like they are saying that the Level 3 definition means that the car handles all aspects of driving but the expectation is that the human driver will respond to a request to intervene.

They are probably referring to this part of the Level 3 SAE definition: "DDT fallback-ready user (while the ADS is engaged) is receptive to a request to intervene and responds by performing DDT fallback in a timely manner." The ADS refers to the Automated Driving System, and the DDT refers to the Dynamic Driving Task. The definition is essentially saying that indeed there must be a human driver that must be ready to intervene and is expected to intervene when alerted by the self-driving car.

But, there is more to this Level 3 definition and I think some of the fake news out there is misreporting it (see my article about fake news and self-driving cars). The SAE Level 3 also says this: "DDT fallback-ready user (while the ADS is engaged) is receptive to DDT performance-relevant system failures in a vehicle systems and, upon occurrence, performs DDT fallback in a timely manner." This portion suggests that the human driver is supposed to in-tune to what the self-driving car is doing, and if the human driver suspects that something is amiss, they as a human driver are supposed to take over the driving controls.

Allow me to make this even clearer, by citing another section of the SAE about Level 3: "In level 3 driving automation, a DDT fallback-ready user is considered to be receptive to a request to intervene and/or to an evident vehicle system failure, whether or not the ADS issues a request to intervene as a result of such a vehicle system failure."

Why am I so insistent on the wording of the Level 3 definition? Here's why. Suppose the human driver of the Audi A8 is led into believing that they can take their eyes off the road, and look at their email, and that they only need to be ready to respond to the self-driving car telling them to take over the controls. Even if we make the rather wild assumption that the self-driving car would tell them to takeover in time to make a decisive and correct action for a pending accident, the issue here is that according to the true definition of Level 3 that the human driver is supposed to somehow know and be ready to take over the car regardless of whether the AI of the car forewarned them or not.

I am betting that by-and-large the human drivers are going to assume that they only need to be ready to take over when notified explicitly by the self-driving car. They will be lulled into believing that the self-driving car knows what it is doing, and that it will prompt them when it is time to takeover. Imagine too the confusion by the human driver that they maybe do notice that the Audi is veering towards danger, but let's assume the Audi's AI system doesn't realize it, and so it is not alerting the human driver. The human driver might be bewildered as to whether he or she should take over the control of the car, and be under the momentary stalled position of not taking over because the self-driving car itself has not said that they do need to take over the control. Am I right to take over the controls when the self-driving car has not told me to do so? You can see this flashing through the mind of the human driver.

Though you might think I am splitting hairs on this, you've got to keep in mind that eventually there is going to be someone driving this alleged Level 3 self-driving car and will get into a car accident that injures or kills someone. An enterprising lawyer will possibly try to find a means to link the aspect that the Audi has a Level 3 capability to the particulars of the accident. This might be something conjured up by a creative lawyer trying to make the case for product liability, or it might be a true aspect that Audi failed to cover as part of the standards of product liability.

As part of a lawsuit, I can envision that there will be expert witnesses involved (I've been an expert witness in cases involving IP in the computer industry), in which these experts will be asked to testify about what the Level 3 capabilities do, how they were developed, the extent of how they work, what kind of testing was done to ensure the features work as claimed, etc.

There will also be a look at how the human driver has been

forewarned about the Level 3 capabilities. What does the Audi user manual say? How easy or hard is it for the human driver to have read the user manual? What was the human driver told by those that sold them the car or rented the car to them? Were they given adequate instructions? Did they comprehend the limitations and what their role is in the driving of the car?

Get yourself ready for the upcoming avalanche of product liability lawsuits regarding self-driving cars. It hasn't happened yet because we are still early in the life cycle of rolling out cars that are used by the public and that have Level 3 and above capabilities. We are still in the old-days of cars that we expect the human driver to be entirely responsible about the driving of the car. With the Level 3 and above, we are blurring the distinction and entering into a new murky era. Where is the dividing line between the human driver responsibility and the self-driving car responsibility? What is the duty of the car maker about identifying that line and making sure that the human driver knows what that line is?

There are those that firmly believe that self-driving cars can do no wrong, or that we must as a society accept that some of the self-driving cars that hit the roads will lead to unfortunate deaths or injuries, but that this is the price we need to pay to ultimately have true Level 5 self-driving cars (under the misguided belief that Level 5 self-driving cars will ultimately eliminate all deaths and injuries, which I've debunked in Chapter 22).

Reality is going to hit those proponents in the face when we have humans getting injured or killed, and when the lawyers say hey, you self-driving car developers and makers, you can't just toss these things into the hands of humans, you need to own up to being responsible for these things. I do dread that day because it will likely dampen the pace of self-driving car advances. On the other hand, I keep exhorting to our industry that we need to put at the head of all this the safety aspects of what we are creating in these self-driving cars. Safety first.

CHAPTER 13

HUMANS COLLIDING

WITH

SELF-DRIVING CARS

CHAPTER 13

HUMANS COLLIDING
WITH SELF-DRIVING CARS

Those darned human drivers!

Yes, that's what the self-driving car community likes to say. They love to put the blame onto those wild and crazy human drivers, especially whenever there is a collision between a self-driving car and a human driven car. Case in point is the Arizona accident in March 2017 that involved a human driven Honda CR-V that collided with an Uber self-driving car. This is a worthy example to take a close look at and be able to predict the future widespread advent of the interaction between self-driving cars and human driven cars. As you will see, in my humble opinion, self-driving cars and the makers of self-driving cars have to wake-up and realize that they cannot simply try to finger point at human drivers. It is the easy way to cop out of ensuring that self-driving cars are truly able to self-drive a car. So far, the public and regulators are so agog over the wonderfulness of self-driving cars that they are buying into the simplistic excuse that human drivers are bad drivers. Eventually, a threshold of pain is going to be reached and the tide will turn against the self-driving cars that aren't able to drive defensively in the same manner that we expect of human drivers.

According to the Tempe, Arizona police investigative report, the human driver of the Honda was trying to make a left turn in an intersection, doing so across three lanes of opposing traffic. In a classic but certainly dangerous maneuver, the human driver observed that the two closest opposing lanes of traffic were backed up with cars, and so the human driver thought they would go ahead and make the left turn into the open gap. Meanwhile, the Uber self-driving car was coming along in the further third lane, and so the Uber car proceeded through the intersection and the human driver rammed into it while making the risky left turn. I think we would all agree that humans that try to make such a left turn are basically risking themselves and others, and it is a type of turn that should be avoided. Sadly, I see human drivers trying this every day, and though they think it is worth the chance, I say they are stupid to do so and that by waiting more patiently they can make the turn without risking everyone. Their impetus to make a risky turn is bad judgement. Period.

That being said, it turns out that the intersection traffic signal had gone to yellow. This of course means that the traffic flowing down that third lane should be cautious as it enters into the intersection. We all know that many people will suddenly floor the accelerator and try to leap through an intersection when the light has gone yellow. Uber claims that the self-driving car did not try to speed-up and jam through the intersection. Instead, they claim that the Uber Volvo was doing 38 mph and was maintaining a constant speed. They also point out that the 38 mph was below the posted speed limit and so the Volvo was not speeding and nor speeding up to make it through the intersection.

The human driver in the Honda plowed into the Uber Volvo and hit so hard that the Volvo veered off into a traffic pole and then flipped onto its side. The Uber engineer that was in the Volvo was miraculously okay and so were all the other humans involved. This could have been a really bad outcome, as you can imagine, given that the occupants in the Volvo could be injured or killed, and the Honda occupants likewise. There could have been a domino effect too, meaning that the Honda could have careened into other cars, and the Volvo could have careened into other cars. In addition, since it involved an intersection, there could have been pedestrians nearby that all could have been injured or killed. By luck, none of that happened, but it could have easily happened and we see in the news this kind of horrific accident involving all human-driven cars all the time.

Let's now unpack what happened in Tempe, Arizona. First, the police say that they are holding the human driver of the Honda at fault, and that the Uber Volvo self-driving car was not at fault. Generally, I think our intuition about driving and the rules of the road allow us to believe that this makes perfectly good sense. The human driver of the Honda took a great risk by making the left turn, and legally they are responsible to only make a left turn when it is safe to do so. Obviously, the outcome shows that it was not a safe maneuver. The Volvo self-driving car had the right to pass through the intersection, regardless whether the light was green or yellow. Had the intersection gone to red, we'd be discussing things differently about why the Volvo went into an intersection that had a red light, and we'd be debating the role of the human driver versus the self-driving car.

Does that mean there's nothing else to discuss? No, not by a long shot. The yellow light of the intersection was presumably viewable by the Uber Volvo self-driving car as it approached the intersection. We all know that you need to gauge your distance to the intersection, your speed, and your ability to make it into and clear the intersection before it goes red. We also all know, as experienced human drivers, that we need to drive defensively and be watching for idiot drivers that are trying to do risky maneuvers. Would a human driver in that Volvo have made the same judgement as the self-driving car and proceeded into that intersection, or would it have decided to brake and instead come to a halt? Or maybe at least slow down and see whether it was truly safe enough to go into the intersection? Especially since the nearby traffic going in the same direction had come to a near halt, which usually we know by experience means that you should be especially watchful of other cars that think this means everything has come to a halt.

We all know too that when you come up to a light that if you suddenly brake or slowdown that there is a danger that an idiot driver behind you might ram into you. They are often not paying attention and so they plow into the back of your car. Or, they are looking at the intersection light and upon seeing it go yellow they want to speed-up, and if you are slowing down it just irks them and they have decided to go faster at the same moment you have decided to go slower. It's a bad combination.

Why didn't the engineer in the Uber Volvo self-driving car take over the controls and provide that kind of human judgement into the situation? The engineer indicated it happened all too fast. I've been pounding away in my series on self-driving cars that this is exactly the problem with self-driving cars that are intended to hand controls over to humans – doing so at the last moment is a false sense of hope and actually often makes things worse. I'll keep making this point until someone hears me emphasizing this.

The point about the AI aspect of the Uber self-driving car is that we really don't know if it had any of this kind of "intuition" about driving a car. I am betting that it simply saw via cameras and radar that the intersection was open and it saw that the yellow light meant it could proceed. I doubt it did much calculation as to the chances of truly clearing the intersection, and I am willing to bet for sure that it did not calculate the aspect of the other lines of cars and the experience laden notion that cars often try to make a left turn across stalled lines of traffic.

Where was the defensive driving of the Uber self-driving car? There seemed to be none. It didn't speed-up and it didn't slow down. It was like the proverbial old granny or grandpa stereotype of proceeding along, merrily, not a care in the world, and just opted to drive right through the intersection. You might say that well, Lance, the Uber self-driving car wouldn't need to drive defensively if we had all self-driving cars on the road, because presumably if the Honda was a self-driving car it would not have attempted to make the risky turn. Hogwash! First, we are going to have a mixture of human driven and self-driving cars for many years to come. I have repeatedly warned that there is not going to be an overnight magic wand that turns all cars into self-driving cars. Second, we don't really know what a self-driving car would have done had it been driving the Honda. If the self-driving car was using machine learning, it might have made similar attempts successfully and thus believe that making the left turn was fine to do, and proceeded exactly in the same manner as the human driver (or, possibly even worse!).

Some witnesses at the scene of the accident say that they thought the Volvo self-driving car did speed-up. Are we to believe Uber that the self-driving car was maintaining speed? So far, it seems like there isn't going to be any further probe into the matter. Wouldn't it be helpful to all self-driving car makers to know more about how this incident occurred, and therefore hopefully be developing their self-driving cars to avoid making the same mistake? You would hope so, but for now, it is unlikely. The excitement and giddiness over the advent of the self-driving car has provide a cloak of supremacy and no one seems to want to dare question what a self-driving car was doing or not doing.

Clearly, if self-driving cars are going to be on the roads, we must expect them to be able to drive defensively. They cannot just move in and around us and not know how to be watchful for the foibles of other drivers. Self-driving cars need to anticipate what human drivers will do. They need to anticipate what other self-driving cars will do. And, keep in mind that not all self-driving cars are doing the same thing. Each self-driving car maker is making their own version of a self-driving car, and so whatever one self-driving car can or cannot do has nothing to do with other self-driving cars. Just as human drivers are distinctive and drive in an individualized manner, so are the various brands of self-driving cars. This regrettably also means that there is no collective learning across all self-driving cars, which, though maybe scary in a big brother way, it would at least potentially allow all self-driving cars to benefit from the experiences of each other.

If self-driving car makers aren't going to infuse defensive driving tactics into their AI, we can likely expect the number of collisions and the human toil to increase. Waiting for machine learning to gradually figure out these circumstances is not the only way to do this. Any experienced driver can tell you about the myriad of ways that they drive defensively. This is both learned and also taught. Most of the self-driving car makers are struggling with just getting their cars to do the usual rules of the road. Venturing into advanced driving techniques such as defensive driving is not something they are yet focused on. In essence, most of the self-driving cars today are about at the level of a high school student that is just learning to drive a car. I'd say it is worse though in many respects because the high school student has the human sensory aspects that the self-driving car lacks, and the high school student has human judgement, even if only that of a naïve teenager.

Defensive driving needs to be more than just avoiding hitting other cars. We need our self-driving cars to be defensive in other ways, such as avoiding hitting motorcyclists. I can vouch that on my daily commute on the freeway, if I strictly drove according to the stated rules of the road, I'd be hitting motorcyclists constantly as they weave into and out of traffic. It takes proper defensive driving tactics to make sure you don't create an accident. For example, all a human car driver would need to do is suddenly switch lanes and then a motorcyclist coming up at a heightened rate of speed would ram right into your car. I've seen this happen to other drivers about three times in the last month alone. It's scary and avoidable. Yes, you can say that perhaps the motorcyclist was reckless, but in the end, reckless or not, the injury and death was brought about by the car that wasn't driving defensively about the reckless motorcycle driver. Fault is one issue, having injury or death is another.

Self-driving cars need to watch out for pedestrians too. I've mentioned in this book that the fatalities of today's human driven cars that pedestrian injuries and deaths due to car accidents has continued to rise. Some believe that self-driving cars will reduce or eliminate these pedestrian incidents. I pointed out that this is not necessarily true, and that we might actually see a further rise once we being to see more self-driving cars on the roads. Self-driving cars can also hit animals, and again this requires defensive tactics to avoid the sudden crossing of a deer or a dog that is chasing a cat across the street. How many self-driving cars are programmed for avoiding that kind of collision? Right now, nearly none.

Those that are developing the AI systems for self-driving cars need to go beyond the aspects of just having automation that drives a car. I agree that being able to have AI that drives a car is huge and a tremendous accomplishment. If the self-driving car was limited to a special track and was guaranteed that there weren't any humans around or near it, I would say that driving a car by AI is sufficient. But, when self-driving cars are allowed among us humans, they must be equipped with defensive driving capabilities. They need to use their sensors to detect circumstances that require specialized driving tactics. They need to be proactive and anticipate dangerous situations. They need to be embodied with practices that can quickly assess a situation and take a course of action to minimize or avoid calamity. This is not easy, but it is a must. It is a must because we cannot assume that an engineer sitting in a several ton vehicle, a potential killing machine, can suddenly take over the controls and avoid collisions. I want self-driving cars as much as anyone else, but not if they are essentially guided missiles that mindlessly are going to be "not at fault" by abiding by strict rules of the road. Let's get some intuition into them and make them savvy AI-based drivers.

CHAPTER 14

ELDERLY BOON OR BUST

FOR SELF-DRIVING CARS

CHAPTER 14

ELDERLY BOON OR BUST
FOR SELF-DRIVING CARS

You probably know about the old saying that a low mileage car driven by an elderly person is a good buy because it has barely been used.

This also goes along with the comedic routines showing a granny or grandpa straining to see over the steering wheel and fearlessly (wildly) driving a car. Other younger drivers often dart around these stereotypical senior citizen drivers. I was even in a car accident years ago wherein someone living at a Leisure World "old folks" home mistakenly used the accelerator when they had meant to use the brake pedal. My car was sitting at a red light when suddenly pow, a car from behind me plowed into my car. The elderly driver was very apologetic and said that she got confused as to which pedal was for what.

I don't want to cast aspersions on older drivers, and we can easily make stereotypical comments about young drivers too (they are reckless, they are distracted by Facebook while driving, etc.). For older drivers, being on-the-road can be very stressful. Someone with failing sight might have a difficult time seeing objects and cars ahead. Night time driving might be especially frightening. Their reactions times to sudden moves of other cars can be delayed. Accidents can happen. Some avoid driving at all. Unfortunately, they then can become trapped at home. They lose their ability to be mobile. This leads often times to losing a sense of identity and a lack of connection to the rest of the world.

Pundits are claiming that self-driving cars will overcome these maladies. Elderly people that otherwise could not drive for themselves, will instead make use of self-driving cars. This will provide them with a new sense of independence. They will join once again the community and be a contributor to society. They will now be able to contribute in special ways such as volunteering their time for schools and charities. They can zip around town by telling the self-driving car to take them to places. Imagine having an always available chauffeur that will take you wherever you want to go. Exciting!

But also a bit of blarney in there too. Let's unpack this notion that self-driving cars is a boon for the elderly. There are certainly some positive aspects, but there are also negative aspects that seem to be left out of the equation. We need to look at both the plusses and the minuses.

First, consider the act of getting into and out of a car. For some elderly, the aspect of getting to the car itself is torturous and sometimes dangerous. If an elderly person has an actual chauffeur of some kind, let's say a young person volunteering to drive the elderly, the young person often helps the elderly person get to and into the car. With a self-driving car, there presumably won't be anyone there to help the fragile get into and out of the car. Certainly there might be someone that can greet an elderly person when they arrive at a destination, and likewise someone helping at the start of a journey. The point though is that the self-driving car is only part of the journey and we need to consider the full set of actions involved.

Next, we are assuming that the cost of the use of a self-driving car is decreased over the cost when having a chauffeur. In other words, presumably today all elderly people could use someone to do their driving, but the cost is prohibitive. How do we know that the cost of self-driving cars will necessarily be as cheap as using a non-self-driving car that has a driver with it? We don't. Most assume that self-driving cars will be the same cost as any other kind of car, but we are likely to see a premium price for self-driving cars, at least for the foreseeable future in the near-term of when this new innovation becomes readily available.

You can expect that marketers are going to realize that having elderly people in self-driving cars is the perfect captive market. Often, elderly have funds they've saved up. You've seen the various ploys used to get them to buy swamp land and other false promising deals. How much will an advertiser pay to show ads to an elderly person that is in a self-driving car and otherwise has no other place to look or hear, other than what is being displayed inside the car? Advertisers will pay plenty. We might even see "free" self-driving cars for the elderly, completely sponsored by hungry advertisers desperate to reach that market segment.

Possible too would be to have the AARP or similar associations that support the elderly becoming sponsors for self-driving cars, or perhaps pushing certain brands of self-driving cars. Car makers would love to get the glow from having an organization like the AARP say that their brand is the only true and trustworthy self-driving car. This would lead the elderly in droves to prefer a particular brand or model of car.

Speaking of trust, one issue is going to be whether the elderly will even trust self-driving cars at all. There are already often jokes made about how the elderly don't know what social media is, or cannot balance their checkbook online. Given their likely suspicious nature of technology, are they really going to be willing to get into a car that has no human driver? Some will, but many won't. Over time, this presumably will even out, in the sense that as self-driving cars become dominant, and as the population ages, you are going to have people that grew-up using self-driving cars that will see the use of self-driving cars as a natural continuation when they get older.

Suppose an elderly person is in a self-driving car, and suddenly the person suffers a stroke? What will the self-driving car do? Will the self-driving car realize what is taking place? The old line about I've fallen down and can't get up, comes to mind. There could be some kind of panic button capability in the self-driving car. Perhaps a voice system that the elderly person can yell and get the AI to realize that something is amiss. The self-driving car might have sensors inside for motion detection and possibly body heat sensors or other biometric detectors. I suppose the self-driving car could even be prepared to drive to the nearest hospital, and perhaps even communicate beforehand to the physicians there that someone is medically in trouble and will arrive in 15 minutes.

We might also see a rise in a new kind of elderly companion, the elderly accompanying passenger. To help the elderly into and out of the car, and assist inside the car as needed, we might have a new occupation of sorts. The person accompanies the elderly and acts as a companion, at least for the journey itself. They talk with the elderly person and interact with the self-driving car, telling the car where to go. This kind of job can be done by someone at minimum wage, and they don't even need a driver's license. They are simply there to be a helper related to the self-driving car and for use by the elderly passenger.

The AI of the self-driving car would need to be adapted to cope with elderly passengers. For example, suppose someone forgets where they intended to go. The AI system might already be familiar with the passenger and "know" where to go. Or, the passenger might get confused and ask to go to the wrong place. The AI system might realize that the desired destination is out-of-place for that person. As a result, the AI might inquire further to make sure, or might even communicate with say a loved one of the elderly person to confirm what the destination should be.

In the near term, we are probably more likely to see that self-driving cars are a "bust" in terms of helping the elderly. It will take a while for the elderly to settle into a comfort zone of using a self-driving car. It will take a while for car makers to hone the self-driving car to this market niche. Eventually, as the population ages and as the AI gets enhanced, the elderly will become more of a boon for self-driving cars. I realize that some of you readers might be offended at this broad generalization about the elderly, so let me be the first to say that there are many elderly that are smarter, sharper, and more alert than many younger passengers and drivers. Don't want to perpetuate any urban myths about the elderly. Nonetheless, it is worth thinking about how the age of the passenger can play into the nature and actions of the AI of a self-driving car. Whether old or young, or in-between, a self-driving car should try to accommodate the particular needs of the passenger.

CHAPTER 15

SIMULATIONS FOR

SELF-DRIVING CARS:

MACHINE LEARNING

CHAPTER 15

SIMULATIONS FOR
SELF-DRIVING CARS:
MACHINE LEARNING

The self-driving car was gradually coming up to a red light at a very busy intersection. Intending to make a right turn, the self-driving car came to a proper stop at the pedestrian walkway and waited to see that it was all clear to make the right turn. Sensing no particular hindrance, the AI instructed the self-driving car to roll forward and make the right turn.

Suddenly, a small child darted off the sidewalk and directly into the path of the self-driving car. Not realizing that the child was going to do this, the self-driving car had little time to react. Upon sensing the movement of the child and having the radar and LIDAR detect that the child was in the way, the AI determined that the only chance of not hitting the child would be to slam on the brakes. Doing so would cause the occupants of the self-driving car to be shaken and possibly suffer neck injuries, but it seemed worth it to avoid hitting the small child. The self-driving car chose to engage the brakes forcibly, but it turns out that meanwhile the small child opted to veer even closer toward the self-driving car and the two struck each other. The child was hit, and the occupants of the self-driving car were also injured. A disaster!

Could this happen? Absolutely. Did it happen? Not in this case, since this was in fact a simulation of a self-driving car and involved trying to teach the AI to be aware of driving situations and what can happen in them. With a computer-based simulation, it is possible to run millions of miles of scenarios for self-driving cars and help the Machine Learning grasp what to do in real-world situations. Google is well-known for having their simulators "teach" their self-driving car software about driving aspects. Nearly all of the prominent self-driving car makers make use of simulations for improving their self-driving car tactics and strategies. Simulators allow us to teach self-driving cars and do so without fear. There is no fear that the self-driving car is going to hurt or kill someone, since it is all taking place in a simulated environment. It is like the movie "The Matrix" for the training of self-driving cars. But, of course, whatever the self-driving car learns during the simulations can ultimately cause harm, if it is learning things that won't properly translate into safe actions while in the real-world.

A simulation for a self-driving car has to be realistic, otherwise it will lead the AI down a primrose path. If the simulator does not abide by the law of physics, for example, and allows a self-driving car to go from 60 to 0 miles per hour in a nanosecond, this is not what happens in the real-world. As much as possible, the simulation has to be equivalent to the real-world. You can't drive up onto the sidewalk willy-nilly to avoid hitting another car. Well, actually, in the real-world you could possibly do so, but you'd need to be sure that going onto the sidewalk was prudent, physically viable, and the only available last-resort option. Some aspects of the real-world are pretty obvious constraints such as not having the self-driving car sprout wings and fly out of a gnarly situation (I am hoping that does become possible at some far ahead future time!), or be able to instantaneously reverse direction or leap over a tall building.

I mention this aspect about needing to have real-world constraints in a simulation since sometimes a self-driving car simulator is based on a car driving game which doesn't especially care about real-world aspects. Many of the car driving games are loosely based on the real-world, but are not "burdened" by having to strictly abide by the real-world. A game that allows the car to hit other cars and bounce off them, or hit pedestrians without caring that those pedestrians are injured or killed would not be an appropriate simulator for machine learning purposes. By extremely careful about using any game playing car simulator when training your self-driving car using machine learning. The machine learning won't realize that those real-world constraints aren't real, and so the AI will ascertain that aspects such as hitting others or flying are all reasonable options to undertake. Keep in mind that the machine learning is looking for patterns and trends, and it will find them in the must subtle of ways, thus, if the simulator doesn't bound it with real-world constraints then it is going to potentially find those "outs" and make use of them whenever it wishes.

At our Cybernetics Self-Driving Car lab, we are using simulators extensively and have some handy tips and insights for others that are desirous of using such simulators.

First, as mentioned, make sure the simulator is based on real-world constraints such as the physics of what happens in the real-world. Objects need to abide by the laws of motion, and need to take into account environmental conditions such as the impacts of rain, snow, and the like. A car reacts differently on a rain soaked road than it does on a dry road. Some simulators don't consider this aspect and so when the self-driving car is trying to learn driving techniques it will falsely think it can hit the brakes and have the same stopping distance no matter what the surface of the road is like. This is not the real-world. This will cause the machine learning to be messed-up in the real-world. Imagine it trying to urgently apply the brakes when driving on an icy road and falsely learned via simulation that the car can stop in a certain distance due to simulations that pretend that all roads consist of pristine asphalt in dry and perfect conditions.

Next, the simulation should have a wide variety of typical driving situations so that the machine learning can properly generalize and find patterns. If the simulator is solely about driving on the open highway, this won't do much good for the machine learning since it will only know about open highway circumstances. It won't know what to do in the inner city or suburb driving conditions. You need to make sure that the simulator covers a myriad of the typical driving situations. Not only is the overall environment crucial, it needs to include aspects such as other cars on the roadway too.

I've seen one simulator that only has the self-driving car on the road. There aren't any other cars. The machine learning will opt to potentially use any lane of the road that it wishes to do so. It can change lanes without having to detect and worry about other cars in those lanes. It can go any speed it wants, since there aren't cars ahead of it. It can brake suddenly and not worry about any cars behind it that might smash into it. This kind of an artificial world is maybe interesting for some research purposes, but it won't help a self-driving car that is destined to be on the real-world roads.

Another simulator that I've seen is one that is skewed in hidden ways. The self-driving car is given the highest priority in the simulator. Thus, if the self-driving car decides to change lanes, and if other cars are next to it, lo-and-behold those other cars let the self-driving car change lanes and don't try to prevent it or get in the way. How many times per day do you try to change lanes and the car next to you always politely lets you do so? Much of the time, another car is going to cut you off, either intentionally since they don't want to let you into their lane, or unintentionally because they didn't even see that you were trying to change lanes. Other cars on the road of the real-world are at times mean and cruel and those car drivers are determined to mess you up. This is what a self-driving car needs to learn about.

Besides having typical scenarios, the simulator needs to be populated by real-world entities. There need to be pedestrians, and they need to be realistic such as darting onto the road when they shouldn't be doing so. There need to be bicyclists and they at times should veer into traffic or make illegal moves. There need to be motorcyclists that drive right next to your car and weave in and out of traffic. As much as possible, the simulator needs to have the same entities as the real-world. Plus, those entities cannot be programmed to be perfect and generous toward the self-driving car. Instead, they need to be programmed to be selfish, inattentive, and have a willingness to do what is wrong as much as they might have a willingness to do what is right.

A really good simulator will also have atypical situations too. During my weekly commute on the freeway, I have seen a motorcyclist get hit about once every two weeks or so. They often straddle the lanes and a car makes a lane change and plows into the motorcyclist. Most of the time, the motorcyclist is able to get up and continue, but sometimes they don't. From a driving conditions perspective, when these incidents occur, the traffic patterns all change as the other cars are jockeying to get out of the way of running over the downed motorcyclist. Also, some cars will stop on the freeway to block other traffic and protect the motorcyclist. Some drivers will pull over to get out of their cars and then offer assistance to the motorcyclist. There are now "pedestrians" essentially on the freeway, which normally a simulator would not include. And so on.

Another aspect of a simulator is whether it provides sensory data for the self-driving car. A real-world self-driving car has sensors such as radar, cameras, and LIDAR (see Chapter 4 about LIDAR). Those sensors are crucial to what the self-driving car is able to detect about the real-world. In most simulators, the simulator is not feeding sensory data to the self-driving car, and instead it is providing other info that is specialized and not part of what sensors would do. The problem here is that the self-driving car is not relying then onto the real-world sensor info, and instead it is being fed some transformed and ready-made info about the traffic and the scene. Again, this is a far cry from what the real-world consists of. Some defend these approaches by saying that the sensory fusion of the self-driving car is a different layer and that the simulator is going above that layer, which I concede, but this is not the same as what actually happens in the real-world.

As an analogy, suppose you were trying to figure out how to use your eyes, your nose, your ears, in order to understand the world around you. Your brain is cognitively trying to comprehend the world, and takes as input the sensory info coming from your eyes, your nose, your ears. If I were to say that I can just plug directly into your brain, and bypass your eyes, nose, and ears, would your mind be learning in the same manner as if it were using your actual senses? Though this might seem like a philosophical debate, it is actually more pronounced as there is definitely a mind-body connection that shapes how we learn and what we learn. A machine learning approach that "learns" without making use of the sensory data that it will be getting in the real-world is gaining a false and misleading perception of the real-world. It will struggle mightily once connected to real-world sensors that are detecting real-world objects and actions.

If you are interested in trying out some of the simulators that exist for training of self-driving cars, here are some notable ones that you might want to use:

Open Source Simulator

Udacity is making available their self-driving car simulator via open source. It was constructed using the free game making tool Unity. You can use the existing tracks and also add new tracks. Go to the Udacity web site or to GitHub and you'll find the simulator available there.

Traffic Simulator

DeepTraffic was made at MIT and provides an ability to simulate highway traffic. It is a means to get your feet wet in terms of neural networks and traffic conditions.

Game Adapted Simulator

Grand Theft Auto (GTA) has been enhanced via OpenAI and the DeepDive Project. Using the Python Universe, the enhanced GTA V provides a 3D world for the exploration of live action and the behavior of people.

Please make sure to keep in mind my aforementioned caveats when using any of these self-driving car simulators. Watch out for non-real-world aspects. Watch out for hidden assumptions embedded deep within the simulator. Watch out for narrow scenarios rather than having a wide diversity of scenarios. Watch out for lack of behavioral aspects and the assumption that other drivers and other people will all be accommodating and polite. Etc.

Real-world testing of self-driving cars is vital to the development of self-driving cars. Taking self-driving cars onto the road and having them experience the real-world is crucial to their maturation. This real-world experience can be aided by the use of simulations. You can do lots of simulations that produce tons of data, and do so at a fraction of the cost of the self-driving car being taken out onto the real roads. It is also obviously safer to use a simulator, while being on the real roads can be dangerous. Also, being on the real roads can be a public relations nightmare for self-driving car makers since whenever a self-driving car makes a mistake it can be captured on video and posted for all the world to see, versus using a simulator and discovering "mistakes" before they happen in the real-world.

That being said, a simulator is not a silver bullet for training the machine learning of self-driving cars. Simulators can only provide so much aid to the AI development for a self-driving car. There needs to be a balance of coupling between training a self-driving car in the laboratory via a simulator, and also simultaneously doing real-world driving. The collection and analysis of real-world driving data helps to make simulators more practical and usable, but it still does not obviate the real-world driving learning itself. Let's make sure our simulators are aiming self-driving cars in the right direction and able to therefore make them more agile and ready for the real-world.

CHAPTER 16

DUI DRUNK DRIVING
BY SELF-DRIVING CARS

CHAPTER 16
DUI DRUNK DRIVING
BY SELF-DRIVING CARS

During Memorial Day weekend, drunk drivers come out in droves. I was on-the-road after attending a beach BBQ, and saw on Pacific Coast Highway (PCH) a car that was weaving back-and-forth across the lanes of traffic ahead of me. He also was sporadically speeding up and then slowing down. Though I could not see the actual driver, his driving behavior was a giveaway that he was likely drunk or as some prefer to say "alcohol-impaired." I opted to remain a sizable distance behind him. Meanwhile, other cars around me weren't willing to stay behind the weaving car and decided to drive past him. As they did so, he nearly swayed over into them. It was a very dangerous situation that was playing out at speeds of 40 to 65 miles per hour.

Statistics in the United States are that about 30 people die in car crashes everyday due to drunk drivers. Sometimes it is reported statistically as there being a drunk driver death every hour. I've covered some of these facets in Chapter 22 about accident driving stats and self-driving cars. Most of the mass media articles about drunk driving and that also touch upon self-driving cars are about how the advent of self-driving cars will presumably do away with any drunk driving related deaths. I debunk this in my other piece. In this piece, I'd like to hone in on a particular facet that no one seems to be willing to talk about, namely when a self-driving car drives like a drunk driver.

I realize you might be taken aback by that statement. How can a self-driving car ever drive like a drunk driver? The self-driving car isn't consuming large quantities of alcohol. It can't go over to the nearby liquor store and get a fifth of scotch. On the surface, my claim that a self-driving car might drive like a drunk driver seems fallacious. We know that a computer is not going to drink alcohol, and so it seems impossible to have a self-driving car wherein the AI is drunk. Well, get ready to have your eyes opened.

At our Cybernetics Self-Driving Cars Lab, we have been exploring what happens when a self-driving car drives in a drunken-like manner.

I am not suggesting that the AI gets drunk, but instead emphasizing that the AI acts in a manner that we associate with drunk driving. For example, in my story about driving down PCH, I mentioned that the car ahead of me was weaving across lanes and sporadically speeding up and slowing down. I could not see the actual human driver, and nor could I give a road sobriety test to the driver. All I knew and could detect was that the car was acting in either illegal ways or at least unsafe ways, and I deduced that likely the driver was drunk. The driver might have been suffering a heart attack and not actually been drunk, or maybe the driver was swatting at a bee that was inside the car and trying to sting him. I don't know for sure he was drunk. I knew for sure that he was driving in a drunken-like manner.

The same can be said of a self-driving car. There are circumstances under which a self-driving car might drive the car in a manner that we would infer implies drunk driving. I know that some advocates of self-driving cars will get very angry with me about this and will fiercely defend that no self-respecting self-driving car would ever drive in an amiss manner. In their utopian world, all self-driving cars are driving perfectly all of the time. What a crock. Even worse is that this kind of claim as made by so-called self-driving car experts is misleading the public and regulators. In the end, this is a ticking time bomb in that ultimately we will realize that self-driving cars can drive like a drunk drivers, and once someone gets hurt by a "drunk driving" AI self-driving car, there will be heck to pay as the public turns sour on self-driving cars and the regulators are forced into putting in place Draconian laws that will disrupt and suppress the progress on self-driving cars.

Why would a self-driving car drive in a drunken manner? There are several ways in which this could readily arise. Let's take a look at the most common ways that this can happen.

Faulty Sensors.

A self-driving car relies upon the sensors that are mounted on and in the car to be able to sense the world around it. These sensors include cameras, radar, LIDAR (see Chapter 4 on LIDAR), and other capabilities. Suppose that a sensor becomes faulty. The sensor fusion by the AI might be misled into believing that there is a car next to it that is trying to come into its lane, and so the self-driving car suddenly changes lanes, even though the other car is not really there (it is considered a "ghost" concocted by the faulty sensor).

This kind of lane changing and speeding up and slowing down could be undertaken by a self-driving car that is getting fed faulty data by its sensors. The AI believes it is doing the right thing and protecting the car and its occupants. Meanwhile, if we were watching the self-driving car, we would think it was drunk driving. We would have no ready way of knowing that the faulty sensors are getting the AI confused. This is analogous to the drunk driver that we don't know for sure is drunk and we need to infer from his wanton behavior that he must be.

Fusion Issues.

The sensory data coming into the self-driving car is being assembled and analyzed via a process often known as sensor fusion. The sensor fusion process consists of piecing together the various sensory data coming from the multiple sensors, and then trying to craft a single comprehensive view of the world around the self-driving car. This requires merging together the radar data coming from several radar devices dispersed around the car, merging together camera images and video streaming coming from cameras mounted all around the car, merging together LIDAR data being collected in 360 degree sweeps, and so on.

Software that is doing the sensor fusion can have bugs in it. These bugs might mislead the system into believing that the outside world is different from reality, and so this is then fed into the AI that has to decide how to drive the car. If the fusion is telling the rest of the AI that there is debris in the roadway up ahead, which maybe is falsely believed based on a mistake in the fusion algorithm, the AI is going to swerve the car to avoid the non-existent debris. From an outside perspective, all that we would see is the self-driving car making an unnecessary radical swerve and we would be perplexed since there was no apparent reason to do so. We'd think it was drunk driving.

Machine Learning False Learnings.

The AI of the self-driving car is often learning about how to drive via the use of machine learning. The machine learning is based on tons of data that is fed into the system. Machine learning can be so complex that we don't know for sure what the system "knows" and nor why it knows what it knows. In a sense, it is like a black box. The behavior of the system is what tells us whether the machine learning is doing a good job or not.

Suppose that the machine learning found a pattern amongst traffic data that suggested that whenever a red colored car was ahead and going more than 80 miles per hour that it was likely that the red colored car will make a rapid lane change into the lane next to it. Based on this trend, the machine learning might then be triggered that if it detects a red colored car that meets that criteria to then take the "safe" action of preemptively making a lane change to avoid having that red colored car merge into it. For those of us observing the self-driving car, we'd have no idea as to why it suddenly opted to change lanes. We might think it was drunk driving.

AI Algorithmic Probabilities and Uncertainties.

Any true self-driving car must contend with probabilities and uncertainties. The real-world of driving is not a one-hundred percent guaranteed situation. Will that pedestrian step off the sidewalk and into the path of the self-driving car? Assign a probability to it, and then the self-driving car will react accordingly. Will that big truck to my right not realize I am in its blind spot and it will try to change lanes into me? Assign a probability to it. There are lots and lots of probabilities and uncertainties involved.

When dealing with probabilities and uncertainties, the self-driving car and its AI is going to take actions based on various thresholds. If it believes that the pedestrian is going to step off the sidewalk, the AI will then take evasive action like instructing the self-driving car to come to a sudden halt. Suppose the pedestrian does not attempt to dart into the street. All that we would see is the self-driving car inexplicably coming to a halt. Bizarre, we might think. Drunken driving, we might ascribe.

Computer Processors and Memory Issues.

The AI that is driving the self-driving car must rely upon lots of computer processors and lots of computer memory to perform all of its calculations and efforts. These processors and their memory are hardware components that can always have the chance of going faulty or failing. Think about your home PC that often runs out of memory and you need to reboot. I am not saying that the processors and memory of the automobile system are the same per se, but merely pointing out that they are hardware and will gradually and eventually breakdown.

If the computer processors or memory go bad, it can impair the AI software. If the AI software is impaired, it might render decisions to the automotive controls of the car that aren't intended. The next thing you know, the self-driving car is making seemingly strange turns and actions that we can't readily explain. Drunk driver.

Internet or External Communications.

Most of the self-driving cars are relying upon external communications such as the Internet to convey aspects of how they are driving to some kind of centralized system. The centralized system is collecting data and using that to do galactic style machine learning that can be shared back to the individual cars and whatever individualized machine learning they are doing.

Imagine that the external communications feeds some kind of instructions into your self-driving car and your self-driving car opts to believe that it should take some kind of evasive action, erroneously, but it doesn't realize it. For example, the centralized system reports that there is a massive pile-up of cars ahead and so get off the freeway right away to avoid it. If we were watching the self-driving car and saw it dart to a freeway exit, we might not know why and would wonder whether it is exhibiting drunk driving behavior.

The aforementioned aspects are all realistic ways in which a self-driving car could be considered to be acting like a drunk driver. The types of actions that we might see include these:

- Swerving across lanes needlessly
- Straddling a lane without apparent cause
- Taking wide turns rather than proper tight turns
- Driving onto the wrong side of the road
- Driving onto the shoulder of the road
- Driving in an emergency lane
- Driving too slowly for the roadway situation
- Driving too fast for the roadway situation
- Nearly hitting another car
- Cutting off another car
- Nearly hitting a pedestrian, bicyclist, or motor cyclist
- Being too close to the car ahead of it
- Stopping when it seems unnecessary
- Rolling past stop signs
- Running a red light
- Other

Any and all of these are actions that a self-driving car might take. The self-driving car might do these actions by intent, meaning that it thought the action was warranted given the existing driving conditions, or it might do it by mistakenly invoking a routine that should not have been invoked. For example, the AI might have a routine or algorithm for purposely driving on the wrong side of the road, which can happen in certain situations, which you as a human driver have undoubtedly encountered. That specific routine could be intentionally or intentionally invoked by the AI, and the next thing you know the self-driving car has gone into the opposing lanes of traffic.

What are we to do about self-driving cars that seem to be drunk driving?

First, we need to make self-driving cars as safe as possible so that they won't do the drunken driving. As I have mentioned throughout this book, this involves ensuring that the sensors have sufficient redundancy and are resilient in the real-world. This requires testing the AI systems to make sure that they will not allow buggy behavior to crop up. This requires layers of safety systems that check and re-check the actions of the AI and the self-driving car and its machine learning, double checking the actions to try and ensure that there is a bona fide reason for the movements made by the system. And so on.

Second, we have to acknowledge that drunken behavior can occur by self-driving cars. There are way too many self-driving car makers that are using the head-in-the-sand approach and pretending that this can never happen. As I have mentioned in this piece, avoiding it is not the answer. In the end, it will happen and it could be the death knell for self-driving cars.

Third, we need to consider the role of the human driver in the self-driving car. I know that most of the self-driving car makers insist that if the self-driving car were to exhibit drunken driving that they assert that the human driver of the car is responsible for the driving of the car and the human driver needs to takeover the controls of the car. This is the case for levels 0 to 4 of self-driving cars (see my article about the Richter scale for self-driving cars levels), but even there it is a misleading and dangerous claim. How is the human driver to know that the self-driving car is making a mistake? Maybe swerving or stopping makes sense to do in a given situation. Even if the human driver realizes that a drunk driving act is occurring, will they be able to react in sufficient time to avoid a calamity?

For level 5 self-driving cars, the viewpoint is that there isn't any means for the human driver to take over control (which I have bashed that idea throughout this book), and so then the human occupants must just hope and pray that the drunken driving self-driving car does not injure or kill them. Without any means to presumably override the self-driving car and its AI, the humans must blindly put their faith into what the self-driving car is doing. This utopian view of self-driving cars is often promulgated by pundits of self-driving cars. It's a scary belief and one that they are deluding themselves and the rest of the world into believing.

Fourth, we have to decide whether or not we want to allow some kind of external control over our self-driving cars. There are some that believe that once we have pervasive V2V (vehicle-to-vehicle communications), we will have self-driving cars that operate as a collective. They communicate with each other and regulate each other. Presumably, in this realm, if a self-driving car detected that another self-driving car was driving drunkenly, it could warn that self-driving car and/or even override what it is doing. Do we want that to happen?

It has both promise and peril. Suppose the other self-driving car is wrong, and it mistakenly or "drunkenly" tells a non-drunk self-driving car to take a bad action?

Likewise, if we have any kind of centralized control of self-driving cars, it can be a boon or it can be an adverse Big Brother. Some believe that police, for example, should be able to take over the controls of self-driving car. Imagine that if bank robbers are trying to get away in a self-driving car, the police could just route the car to a local police station. Of course, the government could potentially use that power for other more nefarious purposes.

Should a drunken driving self-driving car get a DUI ticket? As preposterous as that seems, we do need to consider what will happen when a self-driving car acts in a wanton fashion. We need to have some means to try and get that self-driving car fixed, such as if the sensors are faulty or if the AI is buggy. The occupants of the self-driving car might be blissfully unaware that their self-driving car is acting in this fashion. Hopefully, with the right kinds of on-board detection and safety systems, the self-driving car will alert the occupants that something is amiss. If not, it might be that the police or some authority notifies the occupants that their self-driving car needs to "sober up" and get fixed. In any case, the point here is that we need to be realistic about the aspect that self-driving cars will have the potential for acting in a manner that we would perceive as drunk driving. Let's take precautions to anticipate this outcome.

CHAPTER 17

TEN HUMAN-DRIVING FOIBLES AND

SELF-DRIVING CAR

DEEP LEARNING

COUNTER-TACTICS

CHAPTER 17

TEN HUMAN-DRIVING FOIBLES AND SELF-DRIVING CAR DEEP LEARNING COUNTER-TACTICS

When trying to teach a self-driving car to be on the defense (see Chapter 18 about defensive driving for self-driving cars), it is helpful to provide insightful supervised guidance when the AI is using deep learning, aiding it while the system is figuring out how to deal with roadway traffic. If you feed lots and lots of driving and traffic data into a machine learning algorithm blindly, without any supervision (i.e., unsupervised), it may or may not spot key trends that we already know do exist. Rather than leaving the machine learning algorithm to its own ends and pray that it finds useful patterns, it is appropriate to nudge it toward aspects that will help the automation to ultimately drive a car well and nimbly as it ambles along real-world traveled roads.

Having done an analysis of human drivers and their driving foibles, we can use that analysis to point the deep learning in the appropriate direction. I mention this because there are some self-driving car makers that are pretending that a self-driving car does not have to contend with human drivers that are also on the roadways. These head-in-the-sand developers are envisioning a world in which all cars on the road are only self-driving cars. In this pretend world, the self-driving cars are all polite and civil to each other. They communicate with each other and allow the other car to know where they are going and ensure that no two cars will butt heads. You go, says one car to the other, no you go, says that car in return. What a wonderful world of automation that cooperates with other automation. By banning humans from driving cars, this dream land is one of a utopian car driving nirvana.

Wake-up and smell the roses! This vision is a crock. It will take decades upon decades to get the hundreds of millions of existing cars to eventually become self-driving cars. We are going to have a mix of human driven cars and self-driving cars for the foreseeable future. Some even doubt that we will ever have an all self-driving car environment and that humans will demand that they retain the right to drive a car. That being said, there is the view too that those human drivers will ultimately be overridden by the AI of the self-driving car, when needed, reversing today's roles of the human driver overriding the AI of the self-driving car. In essence, the future is one that allows humans to drive but that the self-driving car knows they aren't that good and so it will take over from them when it chooses to do so. Big brother right there in your own car.

Anyway, facing today's reality of having self-driving cars mixing with human driven cars, we need to ensure that the self-driving car is savvy about human drivers. There is the famous case involving a self-driving car that came up to a four-way stop and came to a proper halt, it then wanted to move ahead, but it saw that a human driven car was also stopped across the intersection. Even though the self-driving car arrived a few seconds before the human driven car, and therefore strictly speaking had the right of way, the human driven car did a classic "rolling stop" (not ever coming to a full stop), and the self-driving car therefore decided to let the human driver go first. Turns out that another human driver did this at the same stop sign, and one after another other human drivers did so, repeatedly, while the self-driving car sat there not moving because it was programmed to let those other cars proceed until it was the self-driving car's turn to go. The self-driving car was playing by civility rules, while the human drivers were gaming the self-driving car. This is the same as if the self-driving car had been a teenager learning to drive, meaning that the more experienced drivers would have taken advantage of the timid teenage driver in a likewise fashion.

What does this tell us? We need to make sure that self-driving cars are wise to the tricks of human drivers. Human drivers have evolved a myriad of cutting-the-corners approaches to driving. Many of these tricks are not particularly legal. On the other hand, they are not so illegal that they can get the human driver readily picked-up and arrested for unsafe driving. Humans have found ways to stretch the boundaries of unsafe driving so that it nears to safe driving, but at the same time when exposed to the glare of proper driving practices it is clearly a lousy and potentially illegal way to drive.

In our self-driving development AI lab, we've been studying how human drivers drive. We then are using large collections of driving data and combining it with guidance to help get the deep learning algorithms to discern patterns involving human driving foibles. We don't need to have the deep learning algorithm start from scratch and wildly look for human driving foibles, which if so would consume tremendous amounts of processing time and might not even find what we know it should be finding anyway. So, we give the deep learning a supervised guidance to get it into the right frame of mind, so to speak. This would be equivalent to sitting with a teenage driver that is first learning to drive, and then pointing out around them the other drivers and the trickery they are doing. You can then have the teenage driver realize how to make sense of a morass of sensory data coming at them, and devise counter-tactics to deal with the human driver foibles.

Some of my AI colleagues have warned me that my self-driving car system might not only learn counter-tactics (which is desired and what I hope to have it learn), but also learn to make use of these human foibles in its own driving. This would seem at first glance to be an adverse consequence of the deep learning. To some degree, though, I am actually seeking for this to happen. Allow me to clarify. I am not aiming to have a self-driving car that drives in an unsafe manner, and nor one that drives illegally. At the same time, you cannot expect a self-driving car that mixes with human drivers to always act in some puritan manner. Let's use the four-way stop example.

At the four-way stop, the self-driving car came to a proper and full stop. It then watched for the other cars to do the same. The other cars were aggressive and inched forward. The inching forward triggered the self-driving car to remain standing still. The self-driving car remained standing still, and one by one the human driven cars did the inching trick. We all do this to each other. The self-driving car could have opted to inch forward, after having made the legal and complete stop, and thusly challenged the other human driven cars. By challenging the other human driven cars, some of those human driven cars would likely have stopped, since they would perceive that the other car is edging ahead. It's a daily game of chicken out there on the roads and byways of the world. A savvy self-driving car needs to know how to play the game of chicken. No more mister nice guy, it's time for the self-driving car to grow-up and put on some boxing gloves.

I include here ten of my favorite human driving foibles. There are more. This is a representative sampling that is illustrative of what it takes to make a self-driving car be savvy and not be a teenage timid and naïve driver.

The Slow Poke

This is a human driver that moves along at speeds that hamper traffic flow. They are often going well below the speed limit. It is as though they cannot seem to find the accelerator pedal. Though not an illegal act, it can be unsafe and cause other traffic to excessively try to get around the slow poke, creating ultimately an unsafe driving situation. This could be ticketed as it is an act that creates a road hazard for traffic. Counter-tactic: The deep learning is guided toward discovering that by detecting ahead of time that there is a slow poke, it is best to switch lanes if possible, prior to coming upon the slow poke. If the self-driving car gets caught directly behind the slow poke, it is now stuck in the slow poke procession and trying to get out will be riskier than if it had avoided getting jammed behind it to be begin with.

The Crazy Lane Changer

This is the human driver that can't seem to find a lane they are willing to stick with. They recklessly jump into one lane, then over into the next lane, then back into the lane they were in. This is often fruitless because of slow traffic that is bumper-to-bumper, but the crazy lane changer appears to be brainless and somehow thinks that rapid lane changes is going to get them faster progress. Not illegal per se, but it creates an unsafe traffic condition that can certainly be ticketed. Counter-tactic: Stay out of the way of the lane changer as they are likely to cut off the self-driving car and leave little or no room for safety. Anticipate which lane they are going into next, and take defensive actions accordingly.

The Cut-You-Off

This is the human driver that opts to push into your lane and do so with just inches to spare in front of you. They cut-you-off. Often, they do this without regard to the safety of others. Sometimes they don't even realize what they have done and are oblivious to other traffic. Counter-tactic: The AI needs to be observant and see if the cut-you-off is doing this ahead of the self-driving car and nearly hitting other cars. If so, the self-driving car needs to be extra careful when nearing the cut-you-off and be ready to slow down, and even be applying the brakes to show brake lights to the cars behind the self-driving car, warning them about a potential sudden stop or slow down.

The No Brake Lights

This is the human driver that either has brake lights that don't work or that opts to not use their brakes (or, uses the parking brake to slow down, which is an old trick used when speeding past a cop and wanting to slow without being obvious of it). Counter-tactic: Self-driving cars are mainly using various distance sensors to detect what the cars ahead are doing. Some also use the camera to read the brake lights of the cars ahead. If using the brake lights as part of the sensor fusion, realize that the brake lights alone are not a sufficient indicator of what the cars ahead will do.

The Lane Straddler

This is the human driver that wants to be in more than one lane at a time, and not simply due to changing lanes. Instead, the human driver straddles two lanes and ends-up blocking both lanes. This is often done on highways when the human driver cannot readily see what the traffic ahead is like because the lane they are in has a big truck blocking their view. They then straddle the other lane, trying to figure out which lane is best to be in. Foolish and unsafe. Counter-tactic: The self-driving car should be cautious when going past the lane straddler, doing so in a lane that the straddler might suddenly decide to occupy. As the self-driving car comes up upon the lane straddler, the self-driving car should be looking for any sideways motions that might suggest the lane straddler is going to veer over into the lane of the self-driving car (and thus the self-driving car needs to adjust accordingly).

The Stutter Stopper

This is the human driver that speeds up, then slows down, then speeds up, then slows down. Maybe they are listening to music on their car radio that gets them to do this. Maybe they do this by some kind of stupid habit. It is annoying and can be unsafe as it confuses other traffic. Counter-tactic: The self-driving car should try to detect the pattern of a stutter stopper and then accordingly plan to start and stop too if behind it, or switch lanes to go around it when feasible to do so.

The Generous

This is the human driver that lets all other drivers cut them off. They are generous to a fault. Though this might seem like a safe way to drive, it actually creates confusion since most other human drivers don't expect it. Then, when they see the generous driver be generous, they insist on getting the same generosity, and if not so provided they then go into reactive driving modes. Counter-tactic: The self-driving car needs to detect the generous driver and either scoot around them or leverage the generosity and make a speed-up or other maneuver to get in front of them.

The Illegal Turner

This is the human driver that seems to believe they can start a right turn from the leftmost lane, or do a left turn from the rightmost lane. They get themselves into a tizzy because the turn they wanted to make is coming due, but they planned poorly for it and make a radical maneuver to make the turn. Counter-tactic: The self-driving car can detect these illegal turners as they usually start to block traffic by slowing way down and then edge into the next lane. By early spotting the behavior, the self-driving car can either give way to let the illegal turner do their thing, or get into a position that prevents the illegal turner from taking action.

The Close Follower

This is the human driver that hugs the car ahead of them. They are within inches of the other car. This allows for insufficient stopping distance. If the car ahead suddenly slams on their brakes, the close follower will end-up in the back seat of the car ahead. Counter-tactic: The self-driving car can usually detect the car follower when it is behind the self-driving car. By making the detection, the self-driving car needs to then purposely drive in a fashion to forewarn the follower about what is going on up ahead. This is an attempt to reduce the car follower surprise if the self-driving car needs to suddenly brake. Another tactic involves moving over into the next lane to let the car follower go past and then be following a car ahead, rather than be following closely the self-driving car.

The Erratic

This is the human driver that appears to be driving drunk. Don't know that the driver is aiming at a DUI, but the way they drive sure seems like it. They speed-up, they slow down, for no apparent reasons, they wiggle around in their lane, they straddle lanes, they don't use their signal when changing lanes, they don't stop at the light and make otherwise erratic moves. Counter-tactic: The self-driving car needs to detect the erratic driver and then give them wide room. Staying back of the erratic driver is sometimes wise, but only safe if giving them lots of distance ahead. Trying to get ahead of the erratic driver might work, but the erratic driver might speed-up and close the gap. The tactic of staying back or moving up ahead depends on the specific erratic nature. Best of all would be to choose a different route and get off the roadway of where the erratic driver is.

The above ten types of human foibles when driving are illustrative of what human drivers do. Their behavior is at times unsafe and can be outright illegal. But this is the way of humans. The ten types were depicted in a fashion that implies one human driver doing the human foible. You can easily have more than one human driven car that is pulling the same stunts at the same time.

In other words, the self-driving car has to anticipate that an erratic driver might be up to their right, and meanwhile a close follower is coming up behind the self-driving car. Furthermore, a lane straddler might be a few car lengths up ahead to the left, and a cut-you-off is rapidly coming from the traffic behind the self-driving car. The AI needs to handle simultaneous instances of each of the various human foible drivers.

This becomes a complicated game of chess. There are several chess boards at the same time, and moves being made by different players. The AI needs to consider the next moves for each of them, and how their moves and the counter-moves of the self-driving car will play out. One human driver can make use of multiple types of bad driving behavior. Multiple human drivers can do so too, in isolation. In addition, multiple human drivers can react to each other, sparking them each to do more of the human foibles.

Today's game playing AI systems are focused on one player at a time kind of strategies. Driving a car involves multiple players and a multitude of strategies. It is also a game of life and death, since whatever the AI decides to do when driving a car can have quite serious consequences. Unlike playing a game of poker or chess, the wrong move can send the self-driving car directly into the path of an erratic human driver and force the two to collide. Waving your hands about the fact that maybe the erratic driver should be considered at fault does little to compensate for someone that gets injured or killed in such a collision. Self-driving cars are the mecca of AI game playing and for those of you that love developing deep learning for game playing, you ought to come over to the self-driving car realm and play the most complicated and serious game there is. Driving a car. It's not so easy.

CHAPTER 18

ART OF DEFENSIVE DRIVING

IS KEY TO

SELF-DRIVING CAR SUCCESS

CHAPTER 18
ART OF DEFENSIVE DRIVING
IS KEY TO SELF-DRIVING CAR SUCCESS

Most of the self-driving car AI capabilities are focused right now on the rules-of-the-road driving practices. Developers are aiming to make sure that a self-driving car will come to a stop at a red light, and that it will abide by the maximum speed limit while going down the road. A self-driving car should stay within its lanes on the freeway. It should react when another car decides to veer into its lane. It is supposed to react if there is suddenly a blown tire laying up ahead and blocking the road. These "reactive" kinds of smarts are crucial for a competent self-driving car.

These reactive practices are the same kinds of tactics that a novice teenage driver first learns when getting behind the wheel. The timid teenager wants to make sure they don't violate any laws and knows that ultimately, they will need to be reviewed by a Department of Motor Vehicles (DMV) official to showcase that they can properly operate a vehicle. The thing is, being a reactive driver is only half of the picture. You cannot always just react to a given situation. Instead, experienced human drivers know that they need to be on the alert to predict and try to avoid dangerous circumstances. We expect human drivers to be able to drive defensively. A defensive driver is one that is constantly scanning the driving environment and trying to anticipate what might go wrong, and anticipate how to best make maneuvers that will hopefully avoid calamities.

Right now, very little attention is going toward true defensive driving for self-driving cars. This somewhat makes sense in that the AI developers are seeking to at least make a self-driving car do what the neophyte teenage driver can do. Once that foundation is established, the goal is to move up the food chain and get the self-driving car to be more like an experienced driver. That being said, having self-driving cars on the roads that are only novice drivers is like driving your car around a bunch of teenage drivers that are just learning to drive. When you see a teenage driver that is barely able to keep a car moving in traffic, you tend to give them wide berth and pray that they don't get themselves into a bad situation. The teenage driver might have the best of intentions as they drive, but without sufficient defensive driving techniques they are likely to produce an accident. The same can be said of the existing self-driving cars. They might have the best of intentions, but their apparent lack of defensive driving skills is going to get someone killed.

Let's use an example of everyday driving to illustrate what I mean by defensive driving. Suppose you are coming up to an intersection and you see that the light is just turning to yellow. You are moving along at say 45 miles per hour and need to decide whether to "go for it" and make the yellow before it goes to red, or whether to come to a halt by braking the car before you enter into the intersection. This happens to you a thousand times a week as you drive around town. Time and again, you are judging whether you should push it and make the light, or whether you should call it quits and come to a stop and wait for the light to go through its next cycle. We generally aren't even explicitly aware that we make these decisions as it has become a routine cognitive game that we have learned by years of driving.

Some human drivers are relatively stupid and simply gauge whether they can make the light or not, and often do not think through the consequences of their decision. Other drivers are more reflective and think about the consequences. For example, if there is a car behind you, you might be thinking about what action they might take related to the yellow light. Suppose you decide to hit your brakes, but the driver behind you doesn't and they are wanting to gun it and make the light, you'll end-up with the car behind you plowing into your car. Or, suppose that there is a car ahead of you, and you are the one that is trying to decide what to do and also anticipate what the car ahead of you is going to do. If you were to make a decision to give the car some added gas to accelerate into the intersection, but if the car ahead of you suddenly slammed on its brakes, you'd be plowing into them.

There are other considerations too. You probably would scan the other lanes that are currently at a red and that are eagerly awaiting the light to go green for them, which will happen when the light goes red to you. Suppose there is a car edging forward and you can see that they are going to try and rush into the intersection the split second that the light goes green for them. You might calculate that it is possible that while you go into the yellow and it turns red halfway while in the intersection that the other car might spring forward and ram into you. There might also be pedestrians that are wanting to cross the intersection, or bicyclists, or motorcyclists. All of these are other "actors" in this driving environment and you need to ascertain what they might do.

A good defensive driver mentally is calculating these factors. The decision to run the yellow or not do so is one that involves measuring the risks of doing so. As a defensive driver, you know that others can take actions that might put you into further risk, especially if you are taking a risk already. These are aspects that a novice teenage driver is not even close to considering. They are simply looking at the yellow light and in a very narrow bandwidth of mental computation trying to decide whether to brake or accelerate to make the light. They don't consider the car ahead of them, the car behind them, the cars waiting to cross from the other direction, the pedestrians, the bicyclists, etc. It is too much for them to consider these aspects all at once. And, in many cases, they haven't even figured out that they should be considering those other factors. Their knowledge of driving is limited to the rules-of-the-road and reactive driving. They have little or no defensive driving capabilities as yet.

Self-driving cars are currently in the same boat, so to speak. They aren't looking at a range of factors and doing proper defensive analyses. In the case of the yellow light, self-driving cars are just like that teenage novice driver. The self-driving car uses its camera to detect the intersection light as yellow. The radar of the self-driving car gauges the distance to the interaction and the distance of the intersection. Using the existing speed of the car, the system calculates whether at its present speed it can reach the intersection and cross through it. If it is going to be tight, the self-driving car AI tries to figure out whether speeding up is possible. Can the car accelerate fast enough, given the distance and however fast the car can speed-up, and make it into the intersection and through it before the red light? If these calculations show that it is not feasible, then the option "obviously" involves braking the car. It is assumed that cars behind the self-driving car will "of course" brake likewise.

In fact, if the humans driving behind the self-driving car did not brake when the self-driving car opted to brake, most AI developers would decry that the stupid human drivers were at fault. The developers would point out that the AI self-driving car made the "right" decision to not run a red light. Those dolt human drivers did not react fast enough to brake and that's their fault. Down with humans! If we only had all self-driving cars then the other self-driving cars behind the car that stopped would have all come to a halt too. Problem solved. Just make sure all cars are self-driving cars.

I've heard this argument so many times and each time it makes me shake my head in exasperation. These AI developers are living in a dream world. Their dream world of all self-driving cars is many years away, likely decades away in time. If they are wanting to have self-driving cars on the roads now, they need to give up on the futuristic utopia and be programming the self-driving car to cope with the realities of being on the road with human drivers. Human drivers are going to be at times dolts, and that's just a fact. It is up to the self-driving car to practice defensive driving tactics. It needs to judge whether the car behind it is likely to stop if it decides to stop. Has the human driven car been riding on the bumper of the self-driving car? Has it shown aggressive driving? These are characteristics that we look for as defensive drivers. Self-driving cars need to do the same. Otherwise, they will be as bad as the teenage novice drivers and produce lots of accidents that could have been avoided.

I'll give you another example of defensive driving, and one that I am sure you've experienced multiple times. Each morning as I am driving to work on the freeway, I drive past a major exit of the freeway that leads to the LAX airport. The exit ramp is miles long and purposely so. Human drivers trying to get to the airport are all scrambling on that exit and often in a panic because they are late for their flight. The volume of cars is tremendous. Eventually, they back-up onto the freeway as there are so many cars trying to get down that exit ramp. Have you seen this kind of driving situation before? Assume so.

Here's where the defensive practices come to play. With the "slow lane" of the freeway now getting clogged by the backed-up cars trying to get down the exit ramp, the other lanes of traffic are meanwhile flowing at 55 to 70 miles per hour. You have cars sitting nearly motionless in the rightmost lane, and immediately next to those cars in the lane next to them are vehicles zipping along at a superfast speed. This is an accident in the waiting. What tends to happen is that a car stuck in the lane trying to exit has a human driver that is upset about the long stationary wait, and so they suddenly try to jump out of the stalled lane and enter into the lane with the zooming traffic.

You then have a car that is going 3 miles per hour that is intersecting with cars that are going 70 miles per hour. These "idiots" often don't consider the fact that they are going to disrupt those fast moving cars. You'll then see the fast moving cars either having to severely brake to avoid hitting the interloper, or they swerve into a lane to the left. But, swerving into a lane to their left causes the cars in that lane to also then be disrupted. Those cars then either start to brake or they swerve too. It is a morning dance that I see each day. It is a dance that typically leads to at least a fender bender at some point, or worse it sometimes leads to horrid accidents and injury or death to those involved in the dance.

If we had a self-driving car that was driving in the lane to the left of the exit lane, and if the self-driving car is not practicing defensive driving tactics, it might be going along in the lane at the maximum speed limit without a car in the world. It "sees" that its lane is open and freely able to proceed. It is not anticipating that a car from the bogged down lane might jump in. As such, when a car jumps into its lane, the move will be unexpected. The self-driving car now has nearly no or limited reaction time. It might not be able to swerve without directly leading to an accident. It might opt to brake but then have cars behind it that ram into the self-driving car.

Had the self-driving car been smart enough to do defensive driving, it might have recognized that there were these stalled cars and determined the chances of a car that might suddenly jump into its lane. It might be already scanning the driving environment and try to find what is the safest path away from any such car that jumps in. The self-driving car might already be tapping its brakes lightly, giving a signal to the car behind it to be watchful that the self-driving car might be needing to brake soon. The self-driving car might decide to proactively move into a lane further to the left and avoid the chances of having a car that jumps into the lane that it was in. These are all prudent defensive driving approaches. Few AI developers are encoding this into self-driving cars currently. Via machine learning, the AI developers are assuming that the self-driving car will figure this out (this is the area of Machine Learning for self-driving cars and the limitations thereof).

The defensive driving that we all take for granted is something that we are partially taught when learning to drive, but it is also learned by the experience of driving. In the case of the LAX exit ramp, if you drove past that several times on successive mornings, you'd gradually see the pattern of cars that come to a halt and then a random number of them that pop over into the next lane to try and extricate themselves from the stalled lane. We cannot just hope that self-driving cars will someday figure this out. We instead need to explicitly make sure that AI developer are fostering defensive driving into self-driving cars, and then in combination make use of machine learning so that the self-driving cars will improve as they drive. We cannot allow self-driving cars onto our roadways that are driving at a novice teenage level and pretend that their lack of defensive driving skills is ok simply because they have a rudimentary capability to navigate the roads. Instead, we have every right and expectation that the self-driving cars are able to drive defensively and avoid accidents or at least try to do so. The art of defensive driving is crucial to all our well-being. May the force be with self-driving cars.

CHAPTER 19

CYCLOPS APPROACH TO SELF-DRIVING CARS IS MYOPIC

CHAPTER 19

CYCLOPS APPROACH TO
TO SELF-DRIVING CARS IS MYOPIC

I recently spoke at an Autonomous Vehicles event and about a week or two beforehand had spoken at another event on Self-Driving Cars. At the first event, there were some fellow speakers arguing that LIDAR is the king and that any self-respecting self-driving car should be "going all the way" with LIDAR (see Chapter 4 covering the LIDAR sensory technology and the controversies about it). Meanwhile, at the second event there was a push by the keynote speaker that Cameras need to be the king of self-driving cars and that LIDAR is over-priced, over-hyped, and just not needed.

This would seem to be quite a confusing predicament to have "experts" claiming that one sensory device is best over another on self-driving cars. The LIDAR-bashing crew showed examples of LIDAR images and challenged the audience to see if it could make any sense out of what the image showed. Audience members were not able to figure out whether a curb existed on the side of the road, and nor whether a sketchy image of a figure was actually a pedestrian or maybe something else like a street post. This seemed to be a very convincing example that LIDAR is no good, it's washed-up, it's got low resolution and ambiguities that make it essentially worthless.

Then, the speaker showed camera-produced street images and asked the audience to see if it could make sense of what was shown. Easily, the audience yelled out that it saw a pedestrian, it saw a curb that was about 4 inches tall, and so on. Wow, this was ample proof that the camera was by far a winner over LIDAR. How could our eyes deceive us? We had seen directly and without any intervention that the camera is better than LIDAR. Case closed.

I was taken aback at such an obvious display of argumentative trickery. Imagine that I was trying to convince you that you should drink milk and that it is overwhelmingly superior to drinking orange juice. I then show you a picture of a person that has been drinking milk and tell you they have all the Vitamin D that they need and their bones are as strong as an ox. I then show you a picture of a person that has been drinking orange juice and they appear weak and brittle. Forget about orange juice, I tell you, not sufficient Vitamin D, so take milk instead.

My answer to this is: Cyclops. Yes, you heard me, I said cyclops. Remember the Greek mythological creature that had a single eye in the center of his forehead? I am calling these efforts to claim that one particular sensory device should be used over another sensory device as the Cyclops Self-Driving Car, and for which I assert that these "experts" are employing a false argument based on the assumption of mutual exclusion. The inherent assumption is that we must for some reason choose between whether to use LIDAR or whether to use cameras. Malarkey. There isn't a valid reason to choose between one or the other. We can have our cake and eat it too. A person can drink milk, getting their Vitamin D, and can drink orange juice, getting their Vitamin C.

Let's take a closer look at the Cyclops argument being used by these self-driving car developers and take it apart.

First, one of the most important aspects of any self-driving car is its ability to undertake sensor fusion. Sensor fusion involves bringing together the sensory data from all sensors on the self-driving car, and fuse it together into something that makes sense. There is live streaming data coming from the cameras on the car, the radar on the car, the LIDAR on the car, and any other sensors such as sensors indicating the speed of the car, the condition of the engine, etc. Each of these sensory devices has a particular viewpoint of what the status of the car is. They need to be assessed and merged into a holistic perspective. The AI of the car needs to ascertain what each sensor is telling it, and which sensor to believe and which one to not believe. For example, if the camera is obscured by dirt and the image is clouded and unusable, the AI needs to then rely upon the radar or some other sensor. If two or more sensors are reporting differing aspects, the AI needs to decide which one is most reliable and most dependable for the particular situation at hand.

Second, let's take the stance that we'll strip the self-driving car of any sensors other than cameras. Guess what, we now have a cyclops. We only have one way to see the world around us. Anything that doesn't go right with those cameras is going to mean that we are blind to the roadway. Driving on a rainy day might cause those cameras to get all smeary with water. With no other sensors to use, the self-driving car is going to be taking some pretty big chances as it drives the road.

Think about how humans and their senses function. You have your eyes, your ears, your nose, your sense of touch, and your sense of taste. Suppose I go around telling you that your eyes are the most important of all senses. You can get rid of those other senses, I tell you. But suppose you go into a dark room and there is a growling angry bear in the corner. You can't see the bear. Seems like your eyes aren't so good for you at that moment. Maybe you should have kept around your ears, just in case. Of course, we can easily come up with valid reasons to have all of our senses and not want to give up any of them.

Third, some might argue that the basis for reducing the sensory devices on a self-driving car is to prevent the AI from getting confused. By having a single form of sensory device, it can just interpret the world in one particular way. For me, that's not a self-driving car that I want to ride in. As mentioned, it will be vulnerable to the capabilities and trade-offs of that one specific type of sensory device. I would much rather have a multitude of sensory devices. I would hope that the AI system would be robust enough to realize what each sensor provides and how to best interpret it. Using an excuse that the AI might be lousy and can't handle more than one sensory device is bottom-line an indication that it is lousy AI and should not be driving that self-driving car.

From a costs aspect, I realize that the more sensory devices we pile onto a self-driving car that the more the costs rise to be able to buy that self-driving car. There is definitely going to be a trade-off between having limited sensory devices and a lower cost self-driving car versus a more robust self-driving car loaded with all sorts of sensory devices. At the same time, we need to think about safety. Will a lower cost self-driving car that has only a few sensory type devices be safe enough to be warrant being on the road and carrying human passengers? I am betting that if such self-driving cars start to become available to consumers, and once they get into a terrible accident or two, we'll see the regulators jump on this design, as will the courts.

You can bet that there will be lawyers that will be happy to line-up and sue those self-driving car makers that opted to use just a single type of sensory device on their vehicles. Did they realize what this would do to heighten risk of death and destruction? Even if they did not realize it, maybe due to having their heads-in-the-sand, an argument could be made that they should have known. As the maker of the self-driving car, they should have considered the risks associated with a cyclops approach. I would guess that nearly any jury would take a dim view of a self-driving car maker that said they were simply trying to bring self-driving cars to the masses. A lofty goal, but minus the safety aspects and you instead have a mass available killing machine.

Overall, I think these advocates trying to push for one sensory device over another are misguided. Some of them do so because they honestly believe in the particular sensory device that they have chosen. They have spent years and years perfecting their understanding of that sensory device. That's great, but it cannot mislead you into thinking that a self-driving car is going to be sufficient with just that one type of a sensory device. A few of those advocates will also begrudgingly concede that other sensory devices can be there too, but they then try to denigrate those other sensory devices, akin to the LIDAR ripping that I mentioned at the start of this piece.

Anybody that knows anything about these sensory devices being used on self-driving cars already knows that each type has its own strengths and weaknesses. We need to have them all on the self-driving car to ensure that we can get a full sense of what is taking place around the car. Sacrificing the ears to have better eyes, or sacrificing the nose to have a sense of touch, these are mutual exclusions that don't make sense for self-driving cars. It is a myopic view to think that we need to only aim at one sensory type.

The initial wave of self-driving cars will be essential to whether the public accepts that self-driving cars are ready for prime time. Cutting corners on the sensory devices will unfortunately make self-driving cars more likely to get into bad accidents, and those bad accidents will turn the tide away from self-driving cars. We'll see the venture capitalists back away from self-driving cars and the media will switch from parading self-driving cars as heroic to instead being villainous death-traps. These sensory device debates are not about adopting VHS versus beta, which some might falsely think, but instead about having a proper and full complement of sensory devices to ensure that highest level of safety when AI is driving that car. Let's put an end to these cyclops self-driving cars, before they hit the roads and start hitting people.

CHAPTER 20

THE STEERING WHEEL GETS SELF-DRIVING CAR ATTENTION AND AI

CHAPTER 20

THE STEERING WHEEL
GETS SELF-DRIVING CAR
ATTENTION AND AI

Like most drivers, you probably don't give much daily thought to the steering wheel in your car. When you first began to drive, the recommended practice was to put both hands on the steering wheel at the 10 o'clock and 2 o'clock positions (that's toward the upper part of the steering wheel, for those of you that don't remember your analog clocks). Nowadays, the 9 o'clock and 3 o'clock positioning is instead the proper handling of your steering wheel, which became recommended due to the advent of air bags and other changes in the mechanical and electronic aspects of modern cars. I am sure though that some of you are still doing the cool-look one-handed 12 o'clock style of driving, which, of course, I must urge you to stop doing and get back to gripping the steering wheel with both hands (for the safety of us all!).

Why the fascination with steering wheels and how to grip them?

Self-driving cars are forcing a reexamination of the everyday steering wheel. There are some self-driving car designs and philosophies that urge auto makers to yank out the steering wheel and all other car controls for self-driving cars, thus preventing the passengers that are inside the car from being able to take control. There is good logic for this notion, and an approach advocated for example by Google. In essence, if a self-driving car is supposed to be able to fully drive a car, why allow the human to suddenly take over the controls and perhaps make a mess of the driving situation. Meanwhile, at the opposite side of this debate, there are some that argue for keeping the controls in the car, especially since a true fully self-driving car is likely many years in the future, and so there will be a need to balance aspects of self-driving by the car with other circumstances wherein the car will need to hand control over to the human, including tricky moments beyond the AI of the car in icy or snowy conditions.

For today's self-driving cars, the steering wheel is actually a key component of the driving equation. Right now, the human driver is still considered the legally responsible driver of the car, and so even if the self-driving element is engaged, ultimately the human driver is supposed to have control of the car. Humans tend to get complacent in these semi-self-driving cars, and take their hands off the steering wheel, along with focusing their attention on that video playing on their smartphone or that sandwich they are trying to eat while driving.

You've perhaps seen the YouTube videos of the Tesla drivers that happily put their hands outside the driver's side window of the car, while it is barreling down the highway at 80 miles per hour. They are supposed to be keeping their hands on the wheel, not waving at passing cows. Tesla has been embattled by some that say that car drivers aren't taking the concept of keeping their hands on the wheel as a serious everyday every moment task. This is why most of the self-driving cars now have some means to alert the human driver to get their hands onto the steering wheel.

The simplest approach to steering wheel engagement by humans involves having a sensor that detects when your hands are on the steering wheel and when they are not. If you take your hands off the wheel for more than a designated amount of time, assuming that the self-driving car is doing the actual driving, the car will emit a tone or buzz to warn you to put your hands back on the steering wheel. This does not mean that you necessarily are now steering car, but just that your hands are ready and able to take over the steering wheel at a moment's notice. Indeed, some self-driving cars will go beyond beeping at you to get your hands onto the steering wheel and will gradually slow down the car, even getting to a full stop, because you refuse to put your hands back onto the steering wheel. This gradual float down to a stop is arguably a dangerous approach and yet it certainly would presumably get the attention of the driver, and one could argue that if the driver has become incapacitated that maybe coming to a proper stop is a prudent safety measure.

Of course, technology should enter into the whole steering wheel topic as a means of helping to solve this problem, and so there are now emerging some new high-tech steering wheels.

For example, at the January 2017 Consumer Electronics Show (CES) in Las Vegas, there were demonstrations of the steering wheels of the future. One steering wheel had not only sensors in it (plenty of them), but it also had a series of LED lights around the circumference of the steering wheel. You can see by the color of the steering wheel whether it is under the self-driving car control or under your human control. You can use various swiping, tapping, and sliding motions on the steering wheel to invoke commands to the car. As you grip the wheel, the LED lights react to your gripping, providing visual feedback to you. When you aren't gripping the wheel, the LED lights provide colors and positions to provide handy visual feedback on the car's status.

Putting more emphasis on the steering wheel seems at first glance a handy way to communicate with the human driver. It is relatively within view since the driver's head should be facing forward anyway. You are sitting upright and can see the steering wheel with general ease. But, some question whether your eyes can really remain on the road, since you now are looking more keenly at the steering wheel, requiring a refocusing of the eyes at something very near, rather than having your eyes scanning the horizon. Furthermore, if the steering wheel has several complex communicative signals, trying to interpret what the steering wheel is trying to flash at you can be cognitively daunting too.

Those that advocate these kinds of communicative steering wheels say that with more AI, and by connecting other aspects such as voice and tactile feel, your efforts to grip the wheel and be provided with relevant on-board car status will become second nature for humans.

Will the steering wheel eventually become a relic of the past? Will you see steering wheels only in museums that display dust-collecting artifacts of the past? Will children ask, what is a steering wheel? Someday we are perhaps headed in that direction. For now, the steering wheel remains a vital part of cars. We take for granted the steering wheel and undervalue its importance. As long as steering wheels are still needed, pushing them forward in terms of their design, capabilities, and with some AI-smarts makes sense. Let's just aim to do so in a manner that keeps our human eyes firmly on the road (along with our minds), even while our hands are on or at least near to the vaunted steering wheel.

CHAPTER 21
REMOTE PILOTING IS
A SELF-DRIVING CAR
CRUTCH

CHAPTER 21

REMOTE PILOTING
IS A SELF-DRIVING CAR CRUTCH

When my daughter was young, I used to take her to the playground and have her go on the swings that were there. Being the classic doting father, I would stand nearby as she went back-and-forth on the swing, wanting to be close enough to catch her if she somehow went astray. Though I tried to look nonchalant about it, she knew that I was hovering and trying to be there to rescue her. Like many youngsters, she was convinced that my rescuer status was unnecessary and in fact that it was inhibiting her from being personally responsible for her own well-being. I admit it was hard to inch away and know that she might get hurt if the swinging got out-of-hand, but it seemed like the prudent thing to do, especially if I wanted her to believe in herself and exercise her own autonomy. Besides, I couldn't always be there at the ready and she would certainly be going on swings someday on her own.

This reminds me about the latest push toward remote piloting of self-driving cars. You might have heard that the California Department of Motor Vehicles (DMV) has been toying with producing a new set of regulations about true self-driving cars in California. Up until now, the regulations in California were aimed at self-driving cars that had a human back-up driver in the vehicle. A true self-driving car is considered a Level 5, meaning that there is no human driver needed since the car is able to do anything that a human driver would be able to do. The AI needs to be as proficient as a human driver. Cars at a less than Level 5 are ones that a human driver needs to be able to take over the driving of the car if needed. Thus, the AI for a less than Level

5 car does not have to be as robust and capable.

Allow me to repeat myself somewhat and emphasize again that a true self-driving car, a Level 5, by definition is a car that can be driven by automation in whatsoever manner that a human driver can. As such, there does not need to presumably be any provision to allow a human to drive the car.

In fact, Google is famous for wanting to eliminate any controls within the car that would allow humans inside the car to try and take over the driving of the vehicle. This is the all-in gambit of the Level 5 car. No controls, no chance of human intervention. Nissan, on the other hand, takes a different approach. They might or might not have controls inside the car, but they are establishing a remote piloting capability to allow humans outside the car to pilot the car, when needed.

California's new DMV draft regulations for true self-driving cars also offers the notion that the car should have a remote capability for humans to engage with the car. I'd like to closely examine this whole topic of remote access to self-driving cars, and take you on a journey about the tradeoffs in this emerging trend.

Let's start at the beginning. There are three major modes involved in remote access to a self-driving car.

Remote monitoring

The simplest mode of remote access is remote monitoring of a self-driving car. In this case, the remote capability allows someone to know whether the car is turned on or not, or whether the car is moving or not, or whether the car has been involved possibly in a crash or not. You might already be familiar with this kind of feature since conventional cars now have this. You can press a button and speak with a human in a faraway remote center, and tell them you are out-of-gas and they'll call for roadside assistance. Or, if you are lonely, I suppose you can just carry on a conversation with another human, with them sitting somewhere in say Nova Scotia, while you are stuck in your car and enduring the daily bumper-to-bumper freeway traffic.

Remote non-piloting control

In this second and more advanced mode, the remotely based human can actually take over some controls of the car, but only in a very limited way. They can for example remotely start the car. They can unlock or lock the doors of the car. Notice that these actions are not associated with the piloting of the car. A remote non-piloting mode is one that allows a remote human to do anything other than actually drive the car. Being able to take action of a non-pilot nature is relatively easy to technologically make happen, and also reduces the amount of skill needed by the remote operator. The remote operator is able to do what the remote monitoring does, and has the added benefit of being able to control non-driving aspects of the car. The range of non-piloting controls can vary quite a bit in terms of particular car models, some of which allow for more or less kinds of non-piloting controls capabilities.

Remote piloting

Finally, there is remote piloting, which is the third and most advanced mode of remote access. In this case, the remote operator can actually drive the car. They are able to turn the steering wheel, apply the brakes, use the accelerator, and overall operate the car. To be able to do so, the car is fitted with various sensor devices such as cameras and distance detectors. The remote operator sits in front of a console and drives the car. You've undoubtedly seen movies that show a remote drone operator piloting an semi-autonomous drone, often in battle scenes where they are viewing a suspect and then launch a missile to get the bad guy.

Now that I've laid out the three modes of remote access, we can take a look at the latest trends in self-driving cars and AI.

I've stated that a Level 5 self-driving car is one that can be operated by AI and do whatever a human can do. If that's the case, would we need a remote piloting capability in a Level 5 car? One answer is no, we would not need a remote pilot since the AI is supposed to be able to fully pilot the car without any needed human intervention. Some argue that well, yes, that's the definition of a Level 5 car, but wouldn't you feel safer to know that a human was able to remotely pilot your car, just in case the AI went haywire or fell asleep at the wheel?

I would argue that I might actually feel less safe if a remote operator took over the controls of my car. Imagine someone that is getting paid minimum wage, and they are sitting in a remote location and driving my car, while I'm in it. Do they really have the needed driving skills? Are they licensed to drive in my particular state? Do they know the rules of the road in my area? Can they really see sufficiently via the camera all the facets needed to safely drive the car? Are they potentially going to be driving my car, while it is on the highway racing along at 65 mph, and maybe suddenly the remote operator reaches for their coffee mug and oops my car goes flying into a ditch?

You might argue that drones are being flown all the time remotely, by both highly trained operators and also by that teenage kid down the street that got one for his birthday. I get that. One little difference. There's no human inside that drone! Of course, the drone can go awry and hit someone, but the point is that currently we aren't allowing human-occupied drones to be piloted remotely publicly. We certainly have the needed technology to be able to remotely pilot cars, trucks, and even planes and ships that have people in them. But, we aren't actively doing so. We still believe in the "human driver inside" aspect.

Nissan is borrowing from NASA (and working with NASA) on the remote piloting of Nissan's self-driving cars. NASA is well known for their remote piloting of vehicles that we land onto other planets. The technology definitely exists. Is it perfected to the degree that we are all Okay with having humans inside the vehicles? That's a big question. And keep in mind that the NASA technology is often millions of dollars of really good high-tech stuff. Car makers are not going to be able to afford having that kind of equipment on your everyday car.

One concern about this movement toward remote piloting is that we are perhaps once again coming back to the human in the equation of driving a car. The AI pursuit is that we are taking the human out of the equation. We want to have cars that drive on a self-driving basis. If we put the human back into the role of driving, this time remotely driving the car rather than driving while inside the car, aren't we also saying that we really don't need the AI to be able to be autonomous? Remember my daughter that wanted me to step away from the swing? If we put in place remote piloting, maybe it reduces our urgency and determination to make self-driving cars that are good enough to really be a Level 5. Remote piloting can be perceived as a crutch and lead to less funding and attention toward the Level 5. We won't reach our desire for truly autonomous drivable cars and trucks if we become reliant on the human-based remote pilot.

Even if you argue that the remote pilot is secondary and that the AI will be the primary driver of the car, this still raises other issues. When will the AI handover control to the remote pilot? When the control is handed-over, will the remote pilot know what is happening? Can the remote pilot react quickly enough? Should the remote pilot be able to take over control from the AI? Under what circumstances? What kind of humans should be allowed to have this kind of life-or-death capabilities and decision making? Will there be regulation to ensure that the remote pilots of cars are properly skilled, trained, and have a track record to proof their reliability? Will this create a security hole that then would allow for hackers to take over your car and drive you to a kidnap spot or worse still aim your car into a brick wall?

For Air Traffic Controllers (ATC's), we require all sorts of stringent conditions on their skills and duties. Right now, the remote pilots for cars are basically whatever a car maker decides they need to be. Suppose we took the same attitude toward air traffic controllers. I don't think any of us would feel safe going up in a plane. This whole topic of the remote pilot labor force is still in its infancy. Mark my words, if we continue along this path, we'll someday maybe have as many remote human pilots of cars as we did when we had phone operators.

I say this because suppose we have millions of cars on the road that are able to be piloted by a remote car operator. Think about how many human pilots you would need to staff for this job. You need to have enough of them to be able to instantly step into driving a car, of which any of those millions of cars on the road might need at any moment. A car that says to you, "we're sorry but all operators are busy," would not be very pleasant when your car is rounding a blind curve and the AI has handed the controls over to the remote center.

In short, this notion of a remote piloting capability sounds good at first glance, but it raises enormous questions about trust. Would you trust your life to a remote human that you don't know and aren't sure that they can pilot your car and that maybe they can't see what your car sees? If the human remote operator suddenly has problems with the camera in your car, and it is all fogged up due to weather, what happens then. Some might also perceive this remote access as a Big Brother kind of aspect, whereby your privacy is being invaded by someone remote. For the remote monitoring, most people that have cars with this feature are not even aware of the possibilities of being remotely spied on. It can happen. For remote piloting, some like the idea because then the police can take over a car being driven dangerously by crazy criminal that is leading a harrowing car chase. Yes, that's true, but the police could also possibly take over your car, even if you are completely innocent. It's a dual-edged sword.

All in all, we need to be on our toes about the remote piloting trend. It does offer a potential safeguard for the advent of self-driving cars, but it is not a silver bullet. By the way, if you are an Uber or Lyft driver, you might want to start playing video games involving driving cars, because soon you might be trading-in your actual car to become a remote pilot for self-driving cars. Just think, no need to dress up anymore, and you can comfortably do your driving while in your pajamas at home. Maybe I should consider that as my next career move.

CHAPTER 22

SELF-DRIVING CARS: ZERO FATALITIES, ZERO CHANCE

CHAPTER 22

SELF-DRIVING CARS: ZERO FATALITIES, ZERO CHANCE

One of the most commonly repeated claims for the advent of self-driving cars is the notion that we will be able to eliminate car related fatalities.

An estimated 30,000 to 40,000 fatalities occur due to car incidents each year in the United States alone. Wouldn't it be wonderful if we could just whisk away those potential future deaths via the miracle of self-driving cars? Presumably, self-driving cars won't get drunk, they won't fall asleep at the wheel, and otherwise won't be subject to the same foibles as human drivers. Indeed, some of the major car makers are saying that with self-driving cars we will have zero fatalities. I say bunk.

There is a zero chance that we'll have zero fatalities due to self-driving cars.

My statement of there being a zero chance might be shocking to some of you. It certainly would be a shock to most of the major media outlets. They have bought into the zero fatalities moniker on a hook, line, and sinker basis. Regulators love the idea too. Self-driving car makers love the idea. Anyone that cares about the lives of people loves the idea. It just sounds catchy and something we all would welcome to have occur. Unfortunately, it is unrealistic and belies the facts.

Let's take a closer look at the fatalities topic. According to the U.S. Department of Transportation (DOT), there were 35,092 fatalities in 2015 due to vehicle related incidents in the United States (DOT census numbers were released in November 2016 and represent the latest counts and statistics available on this topic; we'll need to wait until November 2017 to see the 2016 numbers). They also estimate that it cost about $242 billion dollars for the aftermath recovery of the incidents and fatalities. Obviously, the toll on human lives is huge and so is the monetary cost. Some have argued that if we stopped driving altogether, we could save those 35,000 lives in the United States annually, plus many more globally. They tend to say that we should forget about the use of self-driving cars and just stopping driving cars at all. I'm not going to go down that path here, but you are welcome to look it up and see their position on this.

As a relative comparison, heart disease is the top killer in the United States and amounts to about 614,000 deaths annually. So, the number of car fatalities is relatively small in comparison, and in fact if you add-up the Top 10 means of death in the U.S, the number of car related fatalities amounts to approximately just 1% of that count (it's not even in the Top 10 list). That being said, I want to emphasize that any deaths due to car fatalities is way too much. Anyone that has experienced a friend or family member killed in a car fatality knows the pain and agony associated with car fatalities.

The number of crashes involving those 35,092 fatalities was 32,166. Thus, there were about 1.1 fatalities per crashes involving fatalities. In other words, it tended towards one death, rather than say two or more deaths, on the average overall. The number of motor vehicles involved was 48,923. Thus, there were about 1.5 vehicles involved per crash. This generally seems to make sense, since we would have expected that the fatalities would tend to occur when two or more cars crash together. This is not the only way to have a fatality as it could also be that a car swerves off the road and crashes into a wall, killing someone as a result of the incident and not involving a crash into another vehicle.

We next get into even more interesting stats on the car related fatalities. Consider that a fatality could be the driver of the car, or maybe an occupant inside the car, or perhaps a pedestrian, or a motorcycle rider, or even a bicyclist. Can you guess what percentages each of those circumstances might be? Here's your answer. About two-thirds or roughly 66% were occupants (which includes the driver), while the remaining one-third consisted of pedestrians (16%), motorcyclists (14%), bicyclists (2%), and large truck occupants (2%).

Being a pedestrian is a dicey thing, when it comes to car fatalities, as the number is high enough to realize the potential for getting killed while not actually being inside a car. What we don't know is whether the pedestrians were killed because the driver was essentially at fault, or whether the pedestrian was at fault. In other words, if a pedestrian suddenly darted into the street and there was no reasonable way for the car driver to avoid hitting and killing the pedestrian, this kind of fatality is not particularly attributable to the car and more so to the pedestrian.

Of the occupants killed in the car related fatalities, nearly 52% of the drivers were not wearing their seat belts, while 57% of the passengers were not wearing their seat belts. We don't know how many might have lived had they been wearing their seat belts, but it is generally believed that many, if not even most, would likely have survived the crash. Why is this important? Well, rather than looking toward self-driving cars as a savior to reduce car related deaths, just imagine if we simply got more drivers and occupants to wear their seat belts that we could dramatically likely cut down on the number of car related fatalities immensely.

This is important for another reason too. Let's suppose we do have self-driving cars. The passengers inside the self-driving car should be wearing seat belts as a safety precaution, in case the self-driving car gets into a crash. But, I am willing to bet that people will become complacent and not want to wear their seat belts while in a self-driving car. They will act like they are in a limo or a bus that traditionally you don't wear a seat belt as a passenger. People will tend to trust the self-driving car, over time, and opt to not wear their seat belts. As such, I am predicting that we might actually have a rise of a per capita deaths per self-driving car crash in comparison to non-self-driving car crashes, simply due to people being less likely to wear a seat belt in a self-driving car.

Now, some will say that self-driving cars aren't going to crash. Somehow, magically, the AI in these self-driving cars will prevent the cars from crashing. Really? Let's unpack that logic. If a pedestrian runs into the street and directly in front of a self-driving car, and if there was no practical way for the self-driving car to see or know that the pedestrian was darting into the street, the self-driving car is going to potentially kill that pedestrian (in Chapter 25, I discuss the ethics of self-driving cars and point out that the self-driving car will need to make a choice between harming the car occupants or the pedestrian).

My point is that no matter how good self-driving cars are, you are still going to have circumstances of pedestrians getting killed by accidentally or foolishly getting into the path of the car and when the car itself has no other way to proceed other than killing that person. The same is true of a bicycle rider that swerves in front of a self-driving car. Likewise, a motorcycle rider that goes into the path of the self-driving car. These are plain physics. The self-driving car is not going to magically leap into the air or go into instant reverse. Fatalities are going to happen.

Zero fatalities is zero chance.

Some say that we should focus our attention on engineering and roadway measures, which would separate pedestrians away from cars, any kind of cars, self-driving or human driven. The use of well-designed sidewalks and barriers can likely reduce the pedestrian deaths as much as can the use of self-driving cars.

Another claim about how wonderful self-driving cars will be about reducing fatalities is that self-driving cars don't get drunk. Well, of the 32,166 crashes, there were an estimated 4,946 drunk drivers that were killed. We don't know how many drivers overall were drunk during those crashes, and just know how many of the drivers that were killed had been drunk at the time of the crash. It is predicted that perhaps 6,973 of the deaths could have been avoided if all drivers that were drunk were kept off the roads. Thus, maybe about one-fifth or 20% of the car related fatalities were due to drunk drivers. That's a significant amount, but much less than what is implied by the news media. Most of the general news media seem to think that if we had non-drunk self-driving cars that we'd be down to maybe a handful of fatalities, but as you can see, we'd still have 28,119 deaths. That's a lot.

Of the car related fatalities, about 20% of the deaths are due to the vehicle going off the road and hitting an object, such as a tree, a telephone pole, or other traffic barriers. Why are cars swerving off the road? Could be due to being drunk, could be due to fatigue, could be due to inattention to the task of driving. Some say that we could reduce those deaths by being more careful about putting hardened objects near the roadway. A human driven car would presumably survive if there weren't objects to be hit that would make a crash fatal. One can argue about this, and though some say we should clear the area around roadways or put breakaway objects in their place, it obviously is a rather large logistic problem to somehow make sure that roadways are designed in this manner. But, it is a factor worth considering.

It generally makes sense to believe that a self-driving car is not going to fall asleep or get drunk in any human-like way, but we also should not assume that the AI is perfect and at all times perfect. We all have experienced computer systems that have bugs in them, or where we have hardware fail. Self-driving cars will be no exception. You could be in your self-driving car and suddenly the tires blow, and no matter how good the AI is, the car might go off the road and hit a telephone pole. Or, the AI might encounter a "bug" in the software that causes the car to swerve into a truck next to the car (you might want to read Chapter 9 about the Tesla car that did just that, though the claim is that the software worked as intended and was not a bug per se). Or, the sensors on the self-driving car might suddenly stop working, leaving the self-driving car "blind" to the roadway ahead and it might plow into another car without its sensors being active.

As you can see, there are lots of opportunities for a self-driving car to kill its occupants, or kill pedestrians, or kill bicyclists, or kill motorcyclists. It is going to happen.

We are also somewhat assuming in this false belief about the perfection of the self-driving cars that all cars on the road will be self-driving cars. That's not going to happen for a very long time. We will gradually see self-driving cars emerge. The millions upon millions of human driven cars will exist for years and years. We cannot overnight economically swap out all human driven cars for self-driving cars. As such, you can expect that self-driving cars will be interacting with human driven cars. That interaction is definitely going to produce fatalities.

What then will occur with fatalities and self-driving cars? In some ways, yes, self-driving cars will reduce the fatalities. But, as discussed, in other ways it might keep those fatalities going, and even increase some classes of fatalities. One thing we can say for sure, we aren't looking at zero fatalities simply due to the introduction of self-driving cars. Anyone that says that is living in some kind of science fiction novel. By the time the world gets toward a future of all self-driving cars and relatively perfected AI, we will probably be using our jet packs and maybe even doing Star Trek like beaming, so we might not have conventional car fatalities anymore, and instead have fatality stats on jet pack crashes and beaming problems. Zero fatalities, never. Sorry to break the news to you.

CHAPTER 23

GOLDRUSH:

SELF-DRIVING CAR LAWSUIT

BONANZA AHEAD

Lance B. Eliot

CHAPTER 23

GOLDRUSH: SELF-DRIVING CAR LAWSUIT BONANZA AHEAD

Here's some old jokes that you might enjoy. What's the difference between a lawyer and a leech? The answer is that after you die, a leech will stop sucking your blood. Try this next joke on for size. What's the difference between a good lawyer and a bad lawyer? It is said that a bad lawyer makes your case drag on for years, while a good lawyer makes it last even longer.

I tell these jokes to "jokingly" but also seriously bring up a topic that is an upcoming trend in the self-driving car industry, namely the rise of lawsuits. The self-driving car industry has been relatively lucky so far that the number of lawsuits is modest. As with any industry that begins to attract a lot of money, the march of the lawsuits will come along at the same time. We are seeing daily the emergence of more and more lawsuits aimed at and within the self-driving car marketplace. For the moment, these lawsuits are going to be the bickering and infighting among the self-driving car makers (lawsuits from consumers and buyers and passengers will be the next wave, in about five years, mark my words!).

There's a lot at stake in the development and fielding of self-driving cars. Big money will go to the self-driving car makers. Big money will go to the programmers and AI developers that are at the core of the self-driving cars. Like a gold rush, everyone wants into the action. I've been seeing programmers that have never seen a self-driving car that are revamping their resumes to make it seem like they have twenty years of self-driving car programming experience. There are AI autonomous vehicle researchers at universities that suddenly find themselves no longer hidden in dreary research labs in the basement of the computer science building, and instead have a high-rise corner office with a grand view and are feted by executive assistants that abide by their every command because they have been swooped up by an affluent self-driving car maker.

Here's where the lawsuits are going to come to play. I hire Joe Smith, renowned expert on autonomous vehicles, who has been at the XYZ self-driving car maker, and so he comes to my self-driving car making company with experience under his belt. But, maybe he also comes to me with a slew of design documents and even actual self-driving car code, all of which was developed while at the XYZ company. A boon for my company because I can instantly be already up the learning curve and on par with other companies such as XYZ. Not so good a deal for the XYZ company, which has had its Intellectual Property (IP) "borrowed" and taken to a competitor (some might even say it was "stolen" from them).

The IP ownership question and the use of lawsuits is a recurring theme in the computer industry. Some say that Xerox was the original true owner of the Mac-like interface and that Apple's Steve Jobs ripped off Xerox, and yet Xerox at the time took no direct legal action to recoup this so-called thievery. During the early era of the computer industry the use of lawsuits was less likely, and there was a (some say) naïve view that the computer industry as a whole was benefiting by the sharing and cross-sharing of IP. Had there been zillions of lawsuits, perhaps the computer industry advances would have been stinted and we would not have the miraculous technology that we have today.

Fast forward and there are now lawsuits right and left. The Apple versus Samsung lawsuit over Intellectual Property has been dragging on for years, and the money involved is into the billions of dollars at stake. The issues are so thorny that many of these cases cost millions and millions of dollars to litigate. They even at times make their way to the United States Supreme Court. Businesses are now well aware of their IP, and the need and desire to protect their IP, especially so in high-tech.

Not all cases are legitimate per se.

I might launch a lawsuit over IP that's at a competitor, doing so not necessarily because I believe that I have a proper case, but maybe instead to drain the competitor of their resources and attention, diverting them away from working on systems that are a competition to me. Or, I might do so to strike fear in the hearts of programmers and other AI developers that are maybe thinking of jumping ship over to my competitor.

If I make a big stink by using an IP lawsuit, whether I truly believe in the merits of my case, it can have other handy dampening impacts on other firms. This is especially handy if I am a cash rich firm that can afford to undertake these efforts. Of course, I could also be a tiny startup that maybe finds a hungry attorney that works on a contingency basis and they are willing to take a chance that by suing someone big that there might be a payday. Many of these cases are settled out of court, and so the annoyance factor does get big bucks sometimes to become less annoying or drop the annoyance entirely.

Speaking of IP lawsuits, last week an Intellectual Property lawsuit was filed by the Google self-driving car company Waymo, doing so against Uber. Pause for a moment and read that sentence again. Yes, I just said that two of the biggest and boldest of today's tech firms have decided to go toe-to-toe. Nothing can be more exciting than this. They both have billions and billions of dollars to play with. They can afford the most expensive lawyers. They can play this game with cunning, vast resources, and make it last nearly as long as they want. May the battle of the titans begin!

Here's what the IP lawsuit is about. I preface all this by asking you to use the word "alleged" throughout this discussion of the case, since we don't know the truth of the matter as yet, and right now it is pretty much finger pointing. Anyway, here's the case. Anthony Levandowski had worked at Waymo. He left Waymo. He started up the company Otto, which sought to develop a self-driving truck. The firm Otto was then acquired by Uber. Uber has put Anthony directly into the Uber self-driving vehicle development program. I think those facts seem so far to be undisputed. What Waymo claims is that Anthony downloaded 14,000 files from the Waymo company server, doing so before he left Waymo, and that those files were about self-driving vehicles, and that Anthony then used that to his advantage at Otto, and now Uber also has those to its advantage at Uber (after having bought Otto and brought along Anthony).

Before I say much more about this case, please know that I am not a lawyer, and nor do I play one on TV. I do admit that I have been an expert witness in court cases involving Intellectual Property rights in the computer field. I also have been an arbitrator for the American Arbitration Association involving computer disputes and was certified and served on the computer disputes panel. I also at one time was a university professor and did research with law school colleagues on various facets of the IP and computer industry aspects, publishing some jointly written papers and presenting at conferences. All of this to just suggest that I am an armchair interested party in these kinds of matters.

With those caveats in mind, I believe that we can consider several interesting aspects of this case. First, let's assume that indeed Anthony downloaded the 14,000 files. It might be a lesser number of files, it might be a greater number of files, but the point would be that he downloaded some amount of company files. Why did he do this? Can he somehow justify that while working at Waymo that he had an appropriate basis for doing so?

Next, did he take these files with him to Otto? Maybe he might claim that he did not. He might claim that he left those files at Waymo and walked out the door with nothing more than his own knowledge in his own head. The follow-on logical question would be whether he then took these files over to Uber. Of course, even if he did not, but if he did use them at Otto, then the fruit of the poisonous tree was first born at Otto and Uber is still going to have troubles on its hands.

Suppose the 14,000 files were all about the dining hall at Waymo and consisted entirely of menus and food recipes. If so, and if Anthony really did take the files to Otto and Uber, what adverse impact is there on Waymo due to the taking of the food recipes and menus? One might say that there is nothing that gave Otto and Uber an unfair advantage competitively. Well, Okay, maybe the food recipes led to Otto and Uber improving their own dining halls, and the stomachs of the programmers developing self-driving code were better off because of it.

All kidding aside, presumably the files would need to be pertinent to the self-driving realm to make them a type of taking that has genuinely harmed Waymo. Waymo claims that the files included essentials about LIDAR. LIDAR is an acronym for Light Detection And Ranging, which is a type of hardware and software that uses lasers to do remote sensing. Some self-driving cars are being outfitted with LIDAR and it is a crucial element to being able to detect the surroundings of the self-driving car and integral to the AI and the driving of the self-driving car.

If the files were about LIDAR, this puts those files squarely into the self-driving car realm. Rather than dealing with food recipes, instead now we are talking about key components to making a self-driving car. This is the bloody knife found in the kitchen (that's from the game Clue, for those that don't know). The knife can be a killer weapon and the fact that it is bloody certainly makes it incriminating that it was involved in the murder. Likewise, since Waymo uses LIDAR, and Otto uses LIDAR, and Uber uses LIDAR, it certainly seems like the murder weapon has been found.

Suppose though that Anthony claims he never took the files with him. He might claim that any LIDAR work done at Otto and now Uber is completely separate and apart of what he had been doing at Waymo. Or, he might claim that the work on LIDAR at Waymo was already well known in the industry and was considered common knowledge anyway.

In the case of Tesla, which is currently not making use of LIDAR (Elon Musk prefers cameras and conventional radar), one could potentially try to make the case that the LIDAR doesn't even come to play, though this lawsuit does not involve Tesla and so making that argument in the Waymo and Uber fight won't be particularly applicable. The point though is that if the firm that is accused of exploiting the IP is not even utilizing that type of technology, it would be a bit of an uphill battle to claim clear cut damages to the firm that originally had the IP.

It is too early to predict how this Waymo versus Uber case is going to turn out. We can anticipate that Uber will say the claims are preposterous and try to make it seem like Waymo is just jealous or maybe Waymo is frightened of Uber and so desperate to try and curtail Uber's innovations. We might see Uber countersue Waymo for one thing or another. It will be hard for Uber to make Waymo look like a Goliath trying to squash an innocent David, since both of these firms are giants. Get ready for the fireworks and the tit-for-tat that is going to be a continual stream for years to come. This will be fought as much in the courts as it will be in the media.

There will be legal efforts by Waymo to shut down Uber right away in terms of its self-driving car efforts. Judges will be involved. The legal system will become the fighting ring for these two boxers to duke it out. Will this slow down Uber's efforts? Will this scare others out there at Waymo or other tech firms from not downloading thousands of files and then going across the street to another firm? Will this become a Netflix new series?

Time will tell. What we know for sure is that the lawsuit bonanza is now underway, right or wrong, and so those lawyer jokes that I mentioned earlier should be recast, namely, it is the starting gun for savvy lawyers to start making some money off the jockeying that is going to be taking place in the self-driving car industry. And that's no laughing matter.

CHAPTER 24

ROAD TRIP TRICKERY FOR SELF-DRIVING TRUCKS AND CARS

CHAPTER 24

ROAD TRIP TRICKERY
FOR SELF-DRIVING TRUCKS AND CARS

Let's suppose I tell you that I am going to make a person disappear before your very eyes. That would be quite a magic trick. But, suppose I then say that the person needs to get into this box that I have conveniently placed onto a stage. Well, Okay, that sounds interesting, though it isn't quite the same as having the person just suddenly vanish while standing directly in front of you. Then, I tell you that the person will get into the box and I need to drape a curtain over the box. Then I tell you that you must stand back and cannot inspect the box and nor peek behind the curtain. All in all, I have gone from claiming I could make a person disappear to now having so many qualifications and restrictions that the trick seems a lot less impressive than my original proclamation.

That's exactly what is happening with the various miraculous claims about fully self-driving trucks and cars.

How so? Well, let me take you behind the curtain so you can see how the magic is performed for recent self-driving truck and car headline stories. You'll be somewhat dismayed that recent road trips by so-called fully self-driving trucks and cars are really being done via a bunch of smoke and mirrors. I don't want to seem overly critical about this, but at the same time these efforts to mislead the public and the media are a dual edged sword. On the one hand, it creates rapt attention to the advent of self-driving vehicles and gives us all an exciting jolt about the future. At the same time, it over-inflates what is currently possible and confuses the true status of self-driving and AI capabilities.

You might recall that in October of 2016, an alleged self-driving truck drove one hundred twenty miles across Colorado on their Interstate 25 and delivered 51,744 cans of Budweiser to its destination. This has been touted as the first commercial delivery by use of a fully self-driving truck. The human truck driver was shown sitting in the back cab of the truck and decidedly far away from the driving controls of the truck. They didn't show him drinking any of the 51,744 cans of beer (though, maybe only 51,740 cans of beer made it to the destination, if you get my drift), though they did show him reading the newspaper and otherwise not particularly paying attention to the road. Overall, this was a pretty big splash on headlines across the U.S. and the globe. The future is here. Self-driving trucks are now on the roads and about to take over from all those roughshod truck drivers we see in movies and TV shows.

If you had dug into the particulars about this miracle, you would have noticed the use of hidden smoke and mirrors. Don't read the rest of this piece if you are type that doesn't like spoilers. I am the proverbial magician about to explain how the magic trick was done. Just hope that I don't lose my vaunted magicians license.

First, they had driven that same route beforehand with the human truck driver at the wheel and with the self-driving capability engaged. They did this multiple times. In essence, the self-driving AI capabilities were able to learn about that specific route, over and over. I don't consider this a true self-driving capability in that you would expect any true self-driving AI system to be able to handle a driving route that it has never seen before. Imagine if the only way that your self-driving car or truck could work would be if it had been driven beforehand, several times. Not very practical.

Second, it gets worse in that they tried to keep the driving route exactly the same so that when the self-driving AI system took over there weren't any variants on what it had already seen. How many times have you had a long driving journey that required you to take an alternate route because of an accident on the roadway or perhaps construction taking place? It happens all the time, especially on cross country truck driving. In this case of the Colorado trip, they took great pains to make sure it was as pristine as the first time they did the route.

Third, they had two tow trucks drive the route just before the self-driving truck started on its journey. The purpose of the two trucks was to clear out any stalled vehicles or anything else that would mar the roadway. Really? So apparently, a true self-driving truck or car needs to have idealized roadway conditions? Again, this is just like my earlier indication of making someone disappear before your eyes, but then layering on tons of restrictions and limitations.

Fourth, there were four Colorado State Police patrol cars and three other company vehicles that surrounded the self-driving truck during the trek. They created a cocoon around the self-driving truck. This could ensure that no other cars or trucks on the road could get into the path of the self-driving truck. Imagine a quarterback in a football game completely surrounded by his teammates and no other opposing players could get near, making his run to the goal line about as easy as possible. I realize that you could say that the patrol cars and the vehicles were there for safety purposes, and I get the notion that we would not have wanted the self-driving truck to plow into innocent human-driven cars and trucks. Nonetheless, I really don't see that this cocooning provides much clear-cut evidence that fully self-driving trucks are really here and that this was an example of a truly self-driving truck.

The videos of the journey are at times cleverly shot to portray the self-driving truck without pointing out the cocoon of other protective vehicles around it. For videos that do show those vehicles, you are also not explicitly aware that they are there to brush back anything that might mar the self-driving truck. You are instead led to assume that it was merely to protect other human-driving vehicles, and not so as to try and ensure that the self-driving truck didn't get confused by other human-driven vehicles on the roadway. In real-world driving, we are going to have a mix of human-driven vehicles and self-driving vehicles, thus self-driving vehicles are going to have to know how to deal with the human-driven vehicles around them.

Fifth, the self-driving truck did not do any of the local driving, and only hauled the beer while on the open highway. The human truck driver drove the truck from the loading dock onto the highway, having to navigate all the nuances of city streets and city traffic. Similarly, once the self-driving truck got off the highway at the destination location, the human truck driver once again took the controls. I am sorry to say that I do not consider this to be a true self-driving instance.

Indeed, a true self-driving vehicle is defined as a Level 5 which consists of having the AI system do everything and anything that a human driver can do. From the start of the trip to the end of the trip, a true self-driving vehicle is driven by the AI system and there is never a need for a human driver to take over the controls.

In recap, this alleged instance of a self-driving truck that drove miraculously to deliver beer, actually consisted of a self-driving truck that only drove on the open highway, and only when it was cleared beforehand of any kind of obstructions, and only when surrounded by a cocoon of protective human driven vehicles, and did not drive the entire end-to-end trek and did not encounter anything other than what it had already been able to glean by having repeatedly driven the route beforehand.

Ouch!

I almost feel like this is the famous case of cold nuclear fusion in a jar. Back in the late 1980s, some physicists claimed they could generate nuclear fusion in a jar at room temperatures. The world became ecstatic that inexpensive nuclear energy could be harnessed and so readily made available. Imagine the possibilities and how this would impact society. Ultimately, no one could replicate their claims. It became known as a case of scientific wishful thinking.

The recent spate of road trips with self-driving trucks and cars are very much the same kind of scientific wishful thinking. Those self-driving trucks and cars that we see in glossy videos are not really at the true Level 5 as yet. I believe firmly that we will get there. But we are not there yet, and we still have quite a distance to go. I appreciate that these stunts are helping to spur money and attention toward gaining progress on true self-driving capabilities.

At the same time, I urge us to all carefully look behind the curtain so that we do not get lulled into believing that these capabilities are here when they are not yet here. The next time you see some kind of self-driving truck or car demonstration, don't let them keep you away from the stage, and instead get up into the magical wizardry and make sure that what you are seeing is more than just smoke and mirrors.

I realize it is considered the unspoken ethics of all magicians to not reveal their secrets, but this is a case where I felt the public good outweighed my staying mum on how these seemingly impressive tricks are being performed. I hope to soon be able to say that I saw a self-driving truck or car that did its magic without resorting to any magical trickery. I'll let you know when that happens. Presto!

CHAPTER 25
ETHICALLY AMBIGUOUS
SELF-DRIVING CARS

CHAPTER 25

ETHICALLY AMBIGUOUS
SELF-DRIVING CARS

In 2016, the self-driving car industry was rocked by the crash of a Tesla car that was on autopilot and rammed into a nearby tractor trailer, sadly killing the driver of the Tesla.

This fatal collision gained national and global attention. Some wondered whether this was finally the tipping point that self-driving cars weren't ready for the road and might spark a backlash against the rollout of self-driving cars. For several months, the National Highway Traffic Safety Administration (NHTSA) investigated the incident, utilizing their Office of Defects Investigation (ODI) to ascertain the nature of the crash and what role the human driver of the Tesla played and what role the Tesla Autopilot played.

The ODI announced its results and closed the case on January 19, 2017. Their analysis indicated that they did not identify any defects in the design of the system and that it worked as designed. A reaction by some was of shock and dismay. If the system worked as designed, does this apparently mean that the system was designed to allow it to kill the driver of a car by ramming into a tractor trailer? What kind of design is that? How can such a design be considered ethically okay?

Well, the ODI report explained that the reason the system was "cleared" involved the aspect that the system was designed in a manner that required the continual and full attention of the driver at all times. It was the ODI's opinion that the driver presumably could have taken back control of the car and avoided the collision. Tesla therefore was off-the-hook and the tragic incident was essentially the fault of the driver since he failed to avert the collision.

For Tesla fans and for much of the self-driving car industry, there was a sigh of relief that the self-driving car was not held accountable and nor was the self-driving car maker held responsible for the crash. The self-driving car world got a get-out-of-jail-free card, so to speak, and could continue rolling along, knowing that as long as the system did as it was designed to do, and even if that meant that it either led into a crash and/or did not avoid a crash that it presumably might have been able to avoid, it nonetheless was not to blame in such a severe incident (or, for that matter, apparently for any incident at all!).

Some ethicists were astounded that the self-driving car designers and makers were so easily allowed to escape any blame. Questions that immediately come to mind include:

- Do self-driving car makers have no obligation to design a system that does not lead into a dire circumstance for the driver?

- Do self-driving car makers have no obligation to design a system that detects when a crash is imminent and try to then take evasive action?

- Can self-driving car makers shift all blame onto the shoulders of the human driver by simply claiming that for whatever happens the human driver was supposed to be in-charge and so it is the captain of the ship that must take all responsibility?

This also raises other ethical issues about self-driving cars that we have yet to see come to the forefront of the self-driving car industry. Those within the industry are generally aware of something that ethicists have been bantering around for nearly a hundred years called the Trolley problem. Philosophers and ethicists have been using the Trolley problem as a mental experiment to try and explore the role of ethics in our daily lives. In its simplest version, the Trolley problem is that you are standing next to a train track and the train is barreling along and heading to a juncture where it can take one of two paths. In one path, it will ultimately strike and kill five people that are stranded on the train tracks. On the other path there is one person. You have access to a track switch that will divert the train from the five people and instead steer it into the one person. Would you do so? Should you do so?

Some say that of course you should steer the train toward the one person and away from the five people. The answer is obvious because you are saving four lives, which is the net difference of killing the one person and yet saving the five people. Indeed, some believe that the problem has such an obvious answer that there is nothing ethically ambiguous about it at all. Ethicists have tried numerous variations to help gauge what the range and nature of our ethical decision making is. For example, suppose I told you that the one person was Einstein and the five people were all Nazi prison camp guards that had horribly gassed prisoners. Would it still be the case that the saving of the five and the killing of the one is so easily ascertained by the sheer number of lives involved?

Another variable manipulated in this mental ethical experiment involves whether the train is normally going toward the five people or whether it is normally going toward the one person. Why does this make a difference? In the case of the train by default heading to the five people, you must take an overt action to avoid this calamity and pull the switch to divert the train toward the one person. If you take no action, the train is going to kill the five people. Suppose instead that the train was by default heading toward the one person. If you decide to take no action, you have already in essence saved the five people, and only if you actually took any action would the five be killed. Notice how this shifts the nature of the ethical dilemma. Your action or inaction will differ depending upon the scenario.

We are on the verge of asking the same ethical questions of self-driving cars. I say on the verge, but the reality is that we are already immersed in this ethical milieu and just don't realize that we are. What actions do we as a society believe that a self-driving car should take to avoid crashes or other such driving calamities? Does the Artificial Intelligence that is driving the self-driving car have any responsibility for its actions?

One might argue that the AI is no different than what we expect of a human driver. The AI needs to be able to make ethical decisions, whether explicitly or not, and ultimately have some if not all responsibility for the driving of the car.

Let's take a look at an example. Suppose a self-driving car is heading down a neighborhood street. There are five people in the car. A child suddenly darts out from the sidewalk and into the street. Assume that the self-driving car is able to detect that the child has indeed come into the street. The self-driving car is now confronted with an ethical dilemma akin to the Trolley problem. The AI of the self-driving car can choose to hit the child, likely killing the child, and save the five people in the car since they will be rocked by the accident but not harmed, or the self-driving car's AI can swerve to avoid the child but doing so puts the self-driving car onto a path into a concrete wall and will likely lead to the harm or even death of many or perhaps all of the five people in the car. What should the AI do?

Similar to the Trolley problem, we can make variants of this child-hitting problem. We can make it that the default is that the five will be killed and so the AI must take an action to avoid the five and kill the one. Or, we can make the default that the AI will without taking any action kill the one and must take action to avoid the one and thus kill the five. We are assuming that the AI is "knowingly" involved in this dilemma, meaning that it realizes the potential consequences.

This facet of "knowing" the ethical aspects is a key factor for some. Some assert that self-driving cars and their AI must be developed with an ethics component that will be brought to the fore whenever these kinds of situations arise. It's relatively easy to say that this needs to be done. But if so, how will this ethics component be programmed? Who decides what the ethically right or wrong action might be? Imagine the average Java programmer deciding arbitrarily while writing self-driving code as to what the ethical choice of the car should be. Kind of a scary proposition. At the same time, we can also imagine the programmer clamoring for requirements as to what the ethics component should do. Without stated requirements, the programmer is at a loss to know what programming is needed.

Right now, the self-driving car industry is skirting the issue by going the route of saying that the human driver of the car remains the ethics component of a self-driving car.

Presumably, until self-driving cars get to a true Level 5 of self-driving, meaning that the AI is able to drive the car without any needed human involvement, the existing human driver can still be the scapegoat. I would expect that some clever and enterprising lawyers are eventually going to question whether letting the AI off-the-hook and putting the blame entirely onto the human driver is reasonable, and whether self-driving cars at a level less than 5 can escape blame.

Self-driving car makers don't either realize that they must at some point address these AI and ethics issues, or they are hoping it is further down the road and so no need to get mired into it now. With the frantic pace right now of so many companies striving to get the ultimate self-driving car on the road, their concern is not about the ethics of the car and focused instead on getting a self-driving car that can at least drive the car autonomously.

I see this as a ticking time bomb. The makers think that there is no need to deal with the ethics issues, or they have not even pondered it, but nonetheless it will begin to appear, especially as we are likely to see more fatal crashes involving self-driving cars. Regulators right now have been hesitant to place much regulatory burden onto self-driving cars because they don't want to be seen as stinting the progress of self-driving cars. Doing so would currently be political suicide. Once we begin to sadly and regrettably see harmful car incidents involving self-driving cars, you can bet that the regulators will realize they must take action else their constituents will think they fell asleep at the wheel and will therefore be booted out.

The self-driving car ethics problem is a tough one. Makers of self-driving cars are probably not the right ones to alone decide these ethics questions. Society as a whole has a stake in the ethics of the self-driving car. There are various small committees and groups within the industry that are beginning to study these issues. Besides the difficulty of deciding the ethics to be programmed into the car, we need to also deal with who is responsible for the ethical choices made, whether it be the car maker, the programmers, or some say the car owner because they opted to buy the self-driving car and should have known what its ethics is.

And, suppose that there is agreement as to the ethics choices, and suppose you buy a self-driving car programmed that way, but suppose that the programming of the ethics component did not do as it was intended to do, imagine then having to investigate that aspect. This is a rabbit hole that we are headed down, and there is no avoiding it, so putting our heads in the sand to pretend that the ethics problem doesn't exist or is inconsequential is not very satisfying. Simply stated, the ethically ambiguous self-driving car needs to become the ethically unambiguous self-driving car, sooner rather than later.

APPENDIX

APPENDIX A
TEACHING WITH THIS MATERIAL

The material in this book can be readily used either as a supplemental to other content for a class, or it can also be used as a core set of textbook material for a specialized class. Classes where this material is most likely used include any classes at the college or university level that want to augment the class by offering thought provoking and educational essays about AI and self-driving cars.

In particular, here are some aspects for class use:

o   Computer Science. Studying AI, autonomous vehicles, etc.

o   Business. Exploring technology and it adoption for business.

o   Sociology. Sociological views on the adoption and advancement of technology.

Specialized classes at the undergraduate and graduate level can also make use of this material.

For each chapter, consider whether you think the chapter provides material relevant to your course topic. There is plenty of opportunity to get the students thinking about the topic and force them to decide whether they agree or disagree with the points offered and positions taken. I would also encourage you to have the students do additional research beyond the chapter material presented (I provide next some suggested assignments they can do).

RESEARCH ASSIGNMENTS ON THESE TOPICS

Your students can find background material on these topics, doing so in various business and technical publications. I list below the top ranked AI related journals. For business publications, I would suggest the usual culprits such as the Harvard Business Review, Forbes, Fortune, WSJ, and the like.

Here are some suggestions of homework or projects that you could assign to students:

a) Assignment for foundational AI research topic: Research and prepare a paper and a presentation on a specific aspect of Deep AI, Machine Learning, ANN, etc. The paper should cite at least 3 reputable sources. Compare and contrast to what has been stated in this book.

b) Assignment for the Self-Driving Car topic: Research and prepare a paper and Self-Driving Cars. Cite at least 3 reputable sources and analyze the characterizations. Compare and contrast to what has been stated in this book.

c) Assignment for a Business topic: Research and prepare a paper and a presentation on businesses and advanced technology. What is hot, and what is not? Cite at least 3 reputable sources. Compare and contrast to the depictions in this book.

d) Assignment to do a Startup: Have the students prepare a paper about how they might startup a business in this realm. They must submit a sound Business Plan for the startup. They could also be asked to present their Business Plan and so should also have a presentation deck to coincide with it.

You can certainly adjust the aforementioned assignments to fit to your particular needs and the class structure. You'll notice that I ask for 3 reputable cited sources for the paper writing based assignments. I usually steer students toward "reputable" publications, since otherwise they will cite some oddball source that has no credentials other than that they happened to write something and post it onto the Internet. You can define "reputable" in whatever way you prefer, for example some faculty think Wikipedia is not reputable while others believe it is reputable and allow students to cite it.

The reason that I usually ask for at least 3 citations is that if the student only does one or two citations they usually settle on whatever they happened to find the fastest. By requiring three citations, it usually seems to force them to look around, explore, and end-up probably finding five or more, and then whittling it down to 3 that they will actually use.

I have not specified the length of their papers, and leave that to you to tell the students what you prefer. For each of those assignments, you could end-up with a short one to two pager, or you could do a dissertation length paper. Base the length on whatever best fits for your class, and the credit amount of the assignment within the context of the other grading metrics you'll be using for the class.

I mention in the assignments that they are to do a paper and prepare a presentation. I usually try to get students to present their work. This is a good practice for what they will do in the business world. Most of the time, they will be required to prepare an analysis and present it. If you don't have the class time or inclination to have the students present, then you can of course cut out the aspect of them putting together a presentation.

If you want to point students toward highly ranked journals in AI, here's a list of the top journals as reported by *various citation counts sources* (this list changes year to year):

o   Communications of the ACM

o   Artificial Intelligence

o   Cognitive Science

o   IEEE Transactions on Pattern Analysis and Machine Intelligence

o   Foundations and Trends in Machine Learning

o   Journal of Memory and Language

o   Cognitive Psychology

o   Neural Networks

o   IEEE Transactions on Neural Networks and Learning Systems

o   IEEE Intelligent Systems

o   Knowledge-based Systems

GUIDE TO USING THE CHAPTERS

For each of the chapters, I provide next some various ways to use the chapter material. You can assign the tasks as individual homework assignments, or the tasks can be used with team projects for the class. You can easily layout a series of assignments, such as indicating that the students are to do item "a" below for say Chapter 1, then "b" for the next chapter of the book, and so on.

a) What is the main point of the chapter and describe in your own words the significance of the topic,

b) Identify at least two aspects in the chapter that you agree with, and support your concurrence by providing at least one other outside researched item as support; make sure to explain your basis for disagreeing with the aspects,

c) Identify at least two aspects in the chapter that you disagree with, and support your disagreement by providing at least one other outside researched item as support; make sure to explain your basis for disagreeing with the aspects,

d) Find an aspect that was not covered in the chapter, doing so by conducting outside research, and then explain how that aspect ties into the chapter and what significance it brings to the topic,

e) Interview a specialist in industry about the topic of the chapter, collect from them their thoughts and opinions, and readdress the chapter by citing your source and how they compared and contrasted to the material,

f) Interview a relevant academic professor or researcher in a college or university about the topic of the chapter, collect from them their thoughts and opinions, and readdress the chapter by citing your source and how they compared and contrasted to the material,

g) Try to update a chapter by finding out the latest on the topic, and ascertain whether the issue or topic has now been solved or whether it is still being addressed, explain what you come up with.

The above are all ways in which you can get the students of your class involved in considering the material of a given chapter. You could mix things up by having one of those above assignments per each week, covering the chapters over the course of the semester or quarter.

As a reminder, here are the chapters of the book and you can select whichever chapters you find most valued for your particular class:

ABOUT THE AUTHOR

Dr. Lance B. Eliot, MBA, PhD is the CEO of Techbruim, Inc., and has over twenty years of industry experience including serving as a corporate officer in a billion dollar firm and was a Partner in a major executive services firm. He is also a serial entrepreneur having founded, ran, and sold several high-tech related businesses. He previously hosted the popular radio show *Technotrends* that was also available on American Airlines flights via their in-flight audio program. Author or co-author of six books and over 300 articles, he has made appearances on CNN, and has been a frequent speaker at industry conferences.

A former professor at the University of Southern California (USC), he founded and led an innovative research lab on Artificial Intelligence in Business. Known as the "AI Insider" his writings on AI advances and trends has been widely read and cited. He also previously served on the faculty of the University of California Los Angeles (UCLA), and was a visiting professor at other major universities. He was elected to the International Board of the Society for Information Management (SIM), a prestigious association of over 3,000 high-tech executives worldwide.

He has performed extensive community service, including serving as Senior Science Adviser to the Vice Chair of the Congressional Committee on Science & Technology. He has served on the Board of the OC Science & Engineering Fair (OCSEF), where he is also has been a Grand Sweepstakes judge, and likewise served as a judge for the Intel International SEF (ISEF). He served as the Vice Chair of the Association for Computing Machinery (ACM) Chapter, a prestigious association of computer scientists. Dr. Eliot has been a shark tank judge for the USC Mark Stevens Center for Innovation on start-up pitch competitions, and served as a mentor for several incubators and accelerators in Silicon Valley and Silicon Beach. He serves on several Boards and Committees at USC, including having served on the Marshall Alumni Association (MAA) Board in Southern California.

Dr. Eliot holds a PhD from USC, MBA, and Bachelor's in Computer Science, and earned the CDP, CCP, CSP, CDE, and CISA certifications. Born and raised in Southern California, and having traveled and lived internationally, he enjoys scuba diving, surfing, and sailing.

ADDENDUM

Self-Driving Cars:
"The Mother of All AI Projects"

Practical Advances in Artificial Intelligence (AI)
and Machine Learning

By
Dr. Lance B. Eliot, MBA, PhD

———

For supplemental materials of this book, visit:

www.lance-blog.com

For special orders of this book, contact:

LBE Press Publishing

Email: LBE.Press.Publishing@gmail.com